THIS USED TO BE
CHICAGO

JONI HIRSCH BLACKMAN

Reedy Press
PO Box 5131
St. Louis, MO 63139
www.reedypress.com

Library of Congress Control Number: 2017934679

ISBN: 9781681060910

Cover Photo Attributions
Chicago Fire Engine Co. 18: Courtesy of The Firehouse Art Studio
1949 Chicago Skyline: Courtesy of Associated Press
1960 Chicago Skyline: Courtesy of Associated Press
Coal barge in Chicago River: Courtesy of Library of Congress
Chicago Subway Construction: Courtesy of Associated Press

Printed in the United States of America
17 18 19 20 21   5 4 3 2

CONTENTS

DEDICATION

To my family . . . my children—Beth, Jake (& Jacqueline), Ryan (&
Nikki)—who brought me back to the city, and to Marc, who learned
to love it as I do. To my dad, the Chicago native who suggested I kayak
the Chicago River. To my brother, who photographs us and the city so
beau-tifully. To Abbie Mae who, I hope, someday will chase after me as I
introduce her to what used to be Nana's city.

To all the Chicagoans who fought so hard to keep the buildings so
many cherish. What the East Village Association flyer, written in 1996,
noted about re-developing rather than demolishing the Goldblatt building
can be said about countless others:

"It will require creative thinking and maybe a little time. But in the end,
our community would be better served by protecting the resources we have,
and building for the long-term viability of our neighborhood. Streetscapes
shouldn't be destroyed for a developer's quick buck."

This used to be Dearborn Street—the Monadnock building on the left
and a bit of the old Federal Building across Jackson Boulevard in 1907.
Courtesy of Library of Congress

ACKNOWLEDGEMENTS

My deepest thanks to these people (and probably more). With their help, what used to be a mess of notes is now *This Used to Be . . . Chicago.*

Early editors:
Jennifer Barron, Ann Savage Brown, Ted Slowik, Linda Warner, and John Cygan, my one-time yearbook advisor.

Some fellow Chicago Architecture Foundation docents:
Jim Bartholomew, Betsy Berman, Liz Britt, Jane Buckwalter, Kent Foutty Donna Gabanski, Delta Greene, Harry Hirsch, Larry Kameya, Jack Kremers, Pam Mann, Pris Mims, Roy Slowinski, Lisa Voigt. Also, Tom Martucci, who is not a docent but suggested the MV Abegweit.

Helpful professionals:
Kevin Antene, Natalie Battaglia, Pamela Bannos, Bobby from the Hard Rock Hotel, Jerry Bransfield, Kacey Bogue, Michelle Casini, Beverly Chubat, Jennifer Clement, Curious City for their Motel Row episode, Gia Dragoi, Beth Garneata, Terry Gregory, Ross Guthrie, the very patient Amy Hathaway at the Illinois Historic Preservation Agency, Jennifer Heim, Paul Hirsch, Jacquelyn Jenke, Brian Kallies, John Davies and Dave Truitt and their *Heroes on Deck* documentary, David Kiehn, Dave Kuhlman, and Gail Lawler. Also, Anthony Lowe—the doorman at 1000 W Washington who should write a book, Colby Maddox, Larry Mages, Marilyn from The Bedford, Carli Mason, Mary May, David Meyers, Diane Miskiewicz, Bruce Moffat, Jamie Moncrief, Jayme Nicholas, Jay Nowak, Nick Philp, Todd Regan and Robert Coker, John Ribando, Courtney Ruark, Ali Schwartz, Shayna Swanson, and Johanna Vargas. Also, Michael Svete and Barry Love, who know more about their building than anyone, Cathy Taylor, William Tyre, Danielle Wilcox and the Columbia College buildings website, Duwand Wooden, Sarah Yarrito, Kenton Yoder, and Lili Ann Mages Zisook.

Above and Beyond …

Gladys Alcazar-Anselmo of the East Village Association, Sandy Stylinski —whose father owned the Brundage Building, Gretchen and the other researchers at the Chicago History Museum who encouraged me with their enthusiastic response to my first online inquiry, and the invaluable Barbara Northcott from Reedy Press.

Also, those *Chicago Tribune* reporters whose sometimes very, very old articles en-thralled and informed me; Molly Page, who got me into this … and Hamilton, An American Musical—whose soundtrack got me through this.

Now Metropolitan Place, this modern building was constructed in 1949, designed by Graham, Anderson, Probst & White. This photo was taken in 1978; in 1999, 130 South Canal was converted to retail and residential after four stories were added atop the original six. Courtesy of C. William Brubaker Collection, University of Illinois at Chicago

INTRODUCTION

This Used to Be . . .

I found it completely by accident while looking at street names for another place. I sent a picture to my dad, who remembers living there. I sent a picture of the apartment building that used to be my first home to my dad, who remembers living there. I, who moved in as a newborn and out as a nine-month-old, do not.

A few years after I was born, my dad's company moved into an old paint factory, which was the first building I ever knew of that became something else. Though I spent countless days hanging out there during my youth, I never imagined someday people would live in that somewhat ratty old place. Talking with Tem Horowicz about 1872 N Clybourn was fascinating, as was researching it and eighty-nine other places . . . but then, old newspaper articles are endlessly engrossing to an old newspaper reporter.

The newspapers! Our "first draft of history" provided me an up-close view of what Chicago—not to mention journalism—was like in the late nineteenth and early twentieth centuries. Sometimes I had to laugh and lost count of how many articles claimed these buildings were the BIGGEST, the BEST, the FINEST EVER, ANYWHERE—when they were built.

I developed a deep respect for people like architect Harry Weese, who was so convinced old buildings could be useful places for people to live and work, he introduced some of the first adaptive reuse lofts in Chicago. And for people such as members of the East Village Association who saved the first Goldblatt's, protesting that if they had wanted strip malls, they would have moved to the suburbs.

We used to tease my Chicago-native grandmother when she'd complain something wasn't "like it used to be." But some things, thankfully, can be just like they used to be—and they can remain, as Weese believed, useful. Embracing—instead of erasing—the past builds a city's character . . . and sometimes unearths a few characters in the process.

Enjoy.

Restoration of More Than Hardware

For ninety years, this magnificent building designed by famed Chicago architects Holabird & Roche was the Gold Coast residence of Chicago's Three Arts Club. Modeled after similar women's residential arts clubs in New York, Cincinnati, London, and Paris, members came from every continent to study and work—originally in the "Three Arts" of music, painting, and drama—eventually expanding to newfangled disciplines such as comedy, film, writing, sculpting, and fashion.

Meeting minutes note that in 1921, Robert Frost (with Carl Sandburg tagging along) stopped by (on a snowy evening? Not sure) to read some of his poetry. But no doubt the women of all ages, races, and cultures who lived at the creative sorority-like house for days, or years, were elighted.

The longest-lasting of Three Arts Clubs, it closed in 2004. According to a post on the blog, "The Three Arts Club of Chicago Friends" (May 21, 2009), the more than thirteen thousand women who had lived there over the years were thankful for the opportunity for "time and space for our minds, our creativity . . . contained in a nurturing, safe community in a gently cloistered setting amid one of the world's greatest cultural cities."

It stood empty for years—despite an enticing 2009 offer to turn the building into a columbarium (a place with vaults for the cremated remains of the dead). The quiet, all-residential neighborhood came alive with complaints so vehement, the plan died almost immediately.

The vacant building resonated for Restoration Hardware's Gary Friedman on a 2014 location scouting trip. No property produced goose bumps until this one. "I immediately said, 'I think this is it,'" Friedman told the *Chicago Tribune*, calling the structure "majestic."

Dozens of safeguards assured, reluctant residents finally agreed to the neighbor: RH Chicago includes a coffee and pastry shop, a rooftop park, wine bar, and courtyard cafe.

Anthony Todd of *Chicagoist*: "I'll skip the faux-knowledgeable talk about ceilings and moldings except to say: 'Holy crap, this place is gorgeous.'"

Three Arts' first floor had a drawing room, a grand piano, a library, sitting rooms, a ballroom, a tea room, and a dining room. Courtesy of chicagopc.info

Inset: The North Dearborn Association negotiated thirteen pages' worth of detailed compromises before agreeing to temporary commercial zoning, according to the *Chicago Tribune*. Courtesy of Joni Hirsch Blackman

"No one ever says they want to live in a retail store—until now," said Friedman, perhaps the truest statement ever uttered by a CEO.

That line between home, hospitality, residential, and retail he wanted to blur? Way too hazy to find anywhere in this still-inspirational place.

NOW IT'S...

Was: The Three Arts Club for women

Is: Restoration Hardware's Gallery at the Three Arts Club—lifestyle/showroom/restaurant

Location: 1300 N Dearborn St.

Tip: The stage is original, and though used only to stage furniture, pays homage to the building's former role as an arts-focused residence.

Centuries of Commerce

Once a major department store founded by Abram Rothschild, the "father of the modern department store"—now it's DePaul University's College of Commerce. In 1912, the eleven-story, block-long structure was one of the largest department stores opening on the then-new retail mecca of State Street. Lauded for its Beaux-Arts style, elegant terra-cotta facade and topped with a striking cornice, the 520,000-square-foot structure was on the cutting edge of commerce a century before that was a college subject.

In 1923, A.M. Rothschild & Co. was bought out by Marshall Field's budget-minded subsidiary, Davis Store. In 1936, the Goldblatt brothers—who owned a chain of working-class neighborhood stores—purchased the downtown building and its contents for $9 million. Goldblatt's flagship store anchored State and Jackson for forty-five years, capitalizing on demand for lower-priced retail after the Depression.

But State Street's allure dimmed for mid-1970s shoppers, despite an awkward attempt to turn the former great street into a faux-suburban mall. Goldblatt's was no different than many once-grand department stores attempting to weather the downturn. Some left their downtown buildings, others made adjustments, and some, like Goldblatt's in 1981, filed for bankruptcy.

Snagged by the city for $10 million, the empty store was considered a possible location for the central branch of the Chicago Public Library. Instead, the new Harold Washington Library was constructed diagonally across the street.

Eighty-one years after its construction, DePaul University bought the old discounter at a discounted $1 million in 1991, then spent $65 million renovating it, injecting life into a long-empty stretch of the South Loop.

DePaul Center visitors can cut through the grand interior retail "street" (parallel to State Street) featuring Barnes & Noble and small shops and/or enjoy the outdoor mini-plaza on Jackson.

State Street looking north from Van Buren in the early years of this 1912 structure that was Rothschild's until 1923. Courtesy of Joni Hirsch Blackman.

Inset: Architects Holabird and Roche paid tribute to founder A.M. Rothschild by incorporating the letter "R" into the terra-cotta facade. Courtesy of Kaufmann & Fabry Co.

NOW IT'S...

Was: A.M. Rothschild & Co. Department Store, Davis Store, Goldblatt's

Is: DePaul Center (housing DePaul's College of Commerce)

Location: 333 S State St., at Jackson Blvd.

Tip: Classical medallions with capital Rs inside them (for Rothschild) run along State Street, between the tops of the arches.

As the South Loop now makes obvious, former department stores make excellent college campuses. Seventeen-foot ceilings allow enough space for classrooms with raised seating areas, offering good views of lecturers. The Loop campus's entire library fills the former Goldblatt's tenth floor, a collection that perhaps includes the whole intriguing story of pioneer A. M. Rothschild.

•••

Chicken Soup, Then Basil

It was a hot day during the summer of 1870 when a Lithuanian immigrant showed up for services at a Chicago synagogue wearing a straw hat. City folks, unamused by his casual attire, threw him out. So the hat wearer joined with other immigrants from the old country to establish another house of worship for Chicago Jews. Ohave Sholom Mariampol, at Polk and Dearborn Streets, grew rapidly after 1871's Great Chicago Fire, which brought many newly-homeless Jews into the neighborhood.

In 1892, merging with Anshe Kalvarier—whose building was razed because of the 12th Street/Roosevelt Road widening—the larger congregation was dubbed Anshe Sholom. Still nicknamed "The Straw Hat Shul," the congregation moved to this new building in 1910 at Polk Street and Ashland Avenue.

The Greek Revival-style temple was traditional, with pews upstairs for the women.

It thrived for a decade, but when many in the local Jewish community moved farther west to the Lawndale neighborhood (dubbed "Little Jerusalem"), the synagogue first opened a social center on Homan Avenue and then moved to a new building at Independence and Polk Streets.

On April 9, 1927, the former Anshe Sholom became a Greek Orthodox Church, St. Basil, designated the first Greek Orthodox Cathedral of Chicago by the city's first Greek Bishop. The local Greek newspaper noted more than two thousand people participated in the dedication, six hundred of whom were standing in the aisles.

The building has been scarred by fire twice: once in 1977 and again in 2013. The church was gutted in 1977 but was renovated and reopened. In 1988, the sanctuary was completely renovated.

The University of Illinois's city campus invaded the Greektown area in the mid-1960s, causing church membership to decline. But Medical District, south and west Loop growth has revived the church.

The 1910 Greek Revival-style building was designed by Alexander Levy as a Jewish synagogue. Courtesy of Anshe Sholom

Inset: Moved from Canal Street, becoming "one of the foremost Orthodox groups of the city and a leader in Jewish affairs" according to 1924's *History of the Jews of Chicago*. Courtesy of Beverly Chubat/Meites

The smaller 2013 fire was confined to one corner and took just twenty minutes to put out, but damaged the interior and part of the stained-glass windows.

NOW IT'S...

Was: Anshe Sholom Synagogue

Is: St. Basil Greek Orthodox Church

Location: 733 S Ashland Ave.

Tip: Atop the synagogue, no straw hat—originally a Star of David, later replaced with a crucifix; the original Hebrew letters inscribed beneath remain.

Instituting a Legacy

Phillip D. Armour of meatpacking firm Armour & Company founded Armour Institute with a million dollars in the late 1890s, tapping as its president a minister (Dr. Frank Gunsaulus) who had preached that with $1 million, he could "build a university which would serve all people, not just the elite."

The broad, non-sectarian mission: free and open to all, without any race, creed, or class restrictions.

With only the just-finished Main Building at 1893's opening, Armour offered classes in mechanical, electrical, and mining engineering, though the last was dropped after a year. Added were civil and chemical engineering and—appropriately enough for a city destroyed by a great fire—fire protection engineering, the only course of its kind in the nation in 1903.

Main Building's most striking feature, on the first landing of the main staircase, was donated in 1900—a triptych composed of three stained glass windows with figures representing success, heat, motion, gravity, and light. The windows, designed by Louis Tiffany associate Edwin P. Sperry, were found and refurbished during a 1982 renovation.

Needing more space in 1901, Machinery Hall—with its arched entryway and round-arched windows—opened. Aptly named, the building was designed to handle heavy machinery, housing a machine shop, forge, wood shop, and foundry. An architecture program began as a joint venture with the Art Institute of Chicago. Most unusual were evening classes for working students, a full summer session, and even correspondence courses to serve targeted students. Renamed Armor Institute of Technology in 1895, the school bought its original mechanical and electrical equipment from 1893's World's Columbian Exposition.

In 1940, the Armour Institute merged with engineering college Lewis Institute, forming Illinois Institute of Technology, now known as Illinois Tech. In 2016, officials announced Main Building's conversion to residential apartments, planning to preserve both the vintage stained glass

The two buildings' architects, Patton & Fisher, designed, among other buildings, more than one hundred Carnegie libraries throughout the Midwest.

The former principal classroom facility of Armour Institute was vacant from 2012 until 2017 when MCM Company began to restore and convert the building into apartments. Courtesy of Illinois Tech Courtesy of Illinois Historic Preservation Agency

Inset: The Philip Danforth Armour Institute's second-oldest building, Machinery Hall, was built in 1901 for Mechanical Engineering. Courtesy Illinois Historic Preservation Agency.

windows and the original wrought-iron staircase—not a bad retirement for the hardworking 115-year-old.

NOW IT'S ...

Was: Main Building and Machinery Hall/Armour Institute

Is: Apartments/Illinois Tech

Location: 3300 S Federal St. (Main Building); 100 W 33rd St. (Machinery Hall)

Tip: Both red brick and granite Romanesque Revival landmarks are visible from the Dan Ryan Expressway and the CTA Red Line.

Former White House Occupants' Chicago Home

President Barack and First Lady Michelle Obama bought this red-brick home in 2005 when their two growing daughters made the East View Park condo they'd lived in since 1993 seem a bit cramped. The historically significant, 6,400-square-foot, six-bedroom, six-bath Georgian revival home was built around 1910—much younger and much smaller than the white house in their then-unknown future.

Obama was a junior state senator when they purchased the home and, the following year, part of the adjacent, undeveloped lot. Previously owned by two University of Chicago medical professors, it is situated on a block of similarly historic homes built after the Chicago Fire.

The racially diverse, upscale Hyde Park neighborhood is known for its proximity to the University, as well as for having been the location of the 1893 World's Columbian Exposition and home to the Museum of Science and Industry. The next-most-famous home in the area is Robie House, a Frank Lloyd Wright icon.

After Obama was elected President in 2008, neighbors had to get used to a little drama—Secret Service agents stationed in black SUVs, not to mention the rule requiring neighborhood guests to call ahead before showing up. Street signs reading, "Do not enter this area on foot or by vehicle; this area is protected by the United States Secret Service" were posted.

Whether the former residents will return is top secret. Or maybe they just haven't decided.

This lovely, walkable neighborhood sports one of the former First Family's favorite restaurants: Valois, which features "the Obama Breakfast" on its menu board—items Obama enjoyed when he was a frequent customer.

The home of former President Barack Obama, as seen in 2007. Hyde Park has a history of influential residents—a mix of black and white who are wealthy, well educated, and liberal leaning. Courtesy of AP/Jerry Lai;

Inset: Taken days after the 2008 election, the Chicago home of former President Barack Obama with the added security, street closures, and barricades, as seen. Courtesy of AP/Pablo Martinez Monsivais

NOW IT'S...

Was: President Barack & Michelle Obama's House

Is: A Red (Brick) House

Location: 5046 S Greenwood Ave. (The home has no address but is at the corner of 51st St. (Hyde Park Blvd.) and Greenwood.

Tip: Secret Service agents allow exterior photo-taking from the street, but access into the home or its grounds is prohibited.

Dillinger Was (Literally) Shot Here

It was a movie theater with a cinema-worthy storyline of its own. Genre? True-life crime drama: the death of notorious gangster and "most wanted" criminal John Dillinger.

In 1912, it was just a 125-foot-wide empty lot, purchased by Charles Erickson. Two years later Erickson and his wife, Lena, signed a twenty-year lease with the Lubliner & Trinz movie chain to build a theater of "not less than 999 seats" that the chain would lease for $833.33 a month. Construction of the theater, with adjoining stores, was completed in 1914 but the sheet-metal marquee wasn't added until 1933.

A year later came the theater's "shot" at the big-time. The country's most famous bank robber had been enthralling the depressed nation for thirteen months with fantastical crimes—bank robberies, murders, and several prison escapes. Dillinger's exploits merited banner newspaper headlines and breathless radio dispatches elevating the gangster to folk hero. By June, the new FBI named Dillinger "Public Enemy No. 1," offering a $10,000 reward for his capture.

Dillinger eluded two FBI traps, but the third was the charm. Aided by a North Side madam, Anna Sage, Chicago FBI agent Melvin Purvis knew Dillinger would be at one of two theaters on the night of July 22, 1934, perhaps to see *Manhattan Melodrama* with Clark Gable at the Biograph. Dillinger and two women left the Biograph at 10:45 p.m., walking past Purvis, who signaled waiting officers. When Dillinger reached for a gun, five shots were fired at him. Hit by two, he collapsed, dying before reaching the hospital.

For decades, Biograph management touted a seat in the theater that was supposedly occupied by Dillinger that fateful evening, but in 1967 finally admitted they "don't have any idea what seat he sat in."

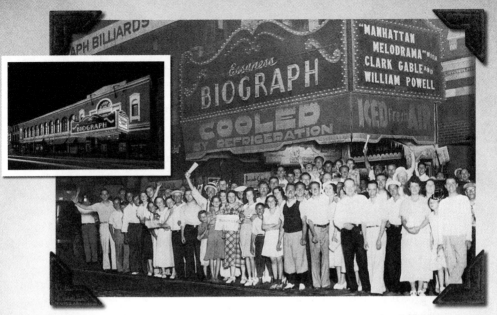

The day after outlaw John Dillinger was shot and killed by federal agents outside the Biograph theater in July, 1934. Hundreds gathered afterward—many reportedly dipped handkerchiefs in his blood on the sidewalk. Courtesy of Associated Press

Inset: The rebuilt marquee looks as it did, except where "Essaness" (the 1930s operator) used to appear, it reads "Victory Gardens." Courtesy of Victory Gardens Theater

NOW IT'S...

Was: Biograph Theater

Is: Victory Gardens Theater at the Biograph

Location: 2433-43 N Lincoln Ave.

Tip: One of Chicago's oldest remaining movie houses and a first-generation movie palace—the only one Dillinger's ghost allegedly haunts.

Infamy continues to bring attention to the Biograph, an excellent example of the earliest movie houses in the country. It was a movie house throughout the 1960s and a four-screen complex from the 1970s until 2001. Victory Gardens, which had been located two blocks south, bought it in 2004, spending two years and $11.8 million rebuilding the entire interior, restoring the grand staircase, and finding original details such as sculptured heads of women ... none related to Dillinger.

One of The Seven

The location is no less lovely than the day investment banker Edward T. Blair "practically decided" to build his town house "just south of Lincoln Park," according to 1912's *Chicago Tribune*. On the empty lot between houses belonging to Victor F. Lawson and Richard T. Crane Jr., Blair "is said to be planning the construction of a beautiful residence. He is now living at the Blackstone (hotel)."

Two years later, the "News of Chicago Society" column described the home, which was designed by "the Blairs' New York architect (who) gave the house a distinctly smart New York air both inside and out. The smooth gray stone, the severe lines and lack of ornamentation of the exterior give it a 'tailor made' look."

The reportedly formal interior had "perfect taste so it interests and impresses the visitor." The gray stone circular staircase led to the second-floor reception room, library, and dining room, described as "spacious and charming." The bedrooms were the "latest word in good taste and luxury combined," where both daughters enjoyed sitting room, bedroom, and bathroom suites.

The twenty-three-room home was sold in 1945 to retailing brothers Louis and Joel Goldblatt, "bachelors who live at the Drake hotel." They sold it two years later to the International College of Surgeons for $85,000; the educational nonprofit group remodeled it at a cost of about $100,000. The house's "imported woodwork . . . hand carved Italian marble fireplaces and doorways" were then noted by the *Tribune*, adding, "the building also has an automatic elevator."

Built in 1914, designed by the architectural firm of McKim, Mead & White, "the residence has been called one of the finest examples of Italian architecture in the country," according to a March 2, 1947 *Chicago Tribune* article.

The left side was originally Blair House, briefly owned later by the Goldblatt brothers. Courtesy of CardCow

NOW IT'S . . .

Was: Blair House, Goldblatts' House

Is: International College of Surgeons (For Sale)

Location: 1516 Lake Shore Dr.

Tip: For sale, $17 million! "Looking for the right owner ready to help re-establish it as an extraordinary single-family residence."

Known as "one of the seven houses on Lake Shore Drive District," the mansion escaped the potential damage that would have ensued in a 1990 attempt to build a luxury condominium atop it. City Hall protests by Gold Coast residents followed and the Commission on Chicago Landmarks denied permits to the potential developer. Bravo!

History Cuts Both Ways —Romantic and Medical

Tabloid sniping is no modern invention—1524 Lake Shore Drive, stately museum now notwithstanding, is proof.

Frederick Countiss met his future wife, Eleanor Robinson, at the home of her father, Diamond Match Co. executive John K. Robinson. At the time, Countiss was engaged to Eleanor's older sister.

But "Eleanor, home from a boarding school for a short vacation, fell in love with her sister's fiancé, and he with her, though she was eighteen years his junior," according to a 1945 *Tribune* article.

The couple, married in 1910, constructed their home in 1917, after, as the museum's website notes, Eleanor's father "generously provided the home building fund." The young woman had a fondness for all things French (in addition to things that belonged to her sister.) Eleanor directed architects to design an elegant Versailles-style French chateau like the one built for Louis XVI and Marie Antoinette . . . apparently not considering how that marriage ended.

Alas, things didn't turn out well for Eleanor and Frederick either. He moved out of their home in February 1923; they divorced two years later amidst voluminous publicity. "Mrs. Eleanor Robinson Countiss . . . prominent socially and noted for her beauty" was declared entitled to "freedom from her marital bonds." The *Tribune* continued, "the news caused no surprise to friends."

Meanwhile, Eleanor's older sister was "happily wed" to a New York millionaire. Just saying.

Eleanor married banker Lawrence H. Whiting two months after her divorce, and in 1931 the forty-three-year-old died after suffering "a nervous ailment which baffled her doctors," according to her obituary.

Meanwhile, Whiting, founder of American Furniture Mart, lived another four decades, years in which the newspapers reported various scuffles

A statue in front of the mansion titled *Hope and Help* is of a doctor holding a sick man; inside, the "Hall of Immortals" displays statues of legendary medical heroes.

Twice the size of neighboring 1516, designed by Howard Van Doren Shaw
and built at a cost of $154,000. Courtesy of Joni Hirsch Blackman

between Whiting and his stepchildren regarding both Eleanor's estate and a
motorboat.

By 1950, Whiting sold the mansion Eleanor loved to the International
College of Surgeons for $185,000 . . . sort of. The college bought it at a tax
sale for $85,000, then Whiting redeemed the property for $85,000, paid the
delinquent taxes from the previous year and resold it to the college. No one
could blame Whiting if he thought, "good riddance!" after unloading the
place, despite the eight marble fireplaces and gilded metal grand staircase.

The museum dedicated to surgical science opened in 1953 after a major
renovation. Sharp remarks now apply more to scalpels than guillotines.

NOW IT'S . . .

Was: Countiss House

Is: International Museum of Surgical Science and
Surgeons Hall of Fame

Location: 1524 N Lake Shore Dr.

Tip: The public museum includes medical art and
a turn-of-the-century apothecary, created from
actual drugstores in New York and Iowa.

Three-Point Powerhouse— Cable Car, Basketball, Pizza

Though San Francisco still has them, Chicago phased out cable cars in 1906, converting to overhead electric lines that were cheaper and more powerful. However, in the 1890s, ours was the largest cable car system in terms of riders and equipment in the country. Thousands of cable cars traveled on more than eighty miles of track over these Midwestern flatlands. Engines ran all those cable cars, including two 300-horsepower Corliss engines located in the Lasalle Street Cable Car Powerhouse.

One engine-powered cable ran through the Lasalle Street tunnel beneath the Chicago River that continued around downtown. The other, shorter cable pulled cable cars along Illinois Street between Clark and Wells Streets. Cable cars carried an estimated 100,000 passengers past the department stores on State Street in the 1890s, and many tourists took cable cars down State Street and Wabash Avenue to the World's Fair in 1893.

This particular powerhouse "was a striking presence in the River North area . . . a jumble of low-scale factories, warehouses and shipyards," said a Chicago Landmarks Designation Report in 2000.

Thousands of Near North-side neighborhood residents took Chicago City Railway cable cars downtown each day in the 1890s and early 1900s—helping spark development of the city's north side neighborhoods during the population boom of the time. An 1889 company brochure notes, "The residents of the North Division are most directly and constantly benefited, and to them the freedom from the bridge nuisance and the advantage of rapid transit are most appreciated, but it is equally true that nine-tenths of the visitors to Lincoln Park . . . are patrons of the North Chicago Street Railroad Company."

Years before today's L circled downtown, Chicago City Railway's ground-level cable car system traced a Loop as it ran along its four streets: (Wabash Avenue, State, Madison, and Lake Streets) in 1882.

One of three powerhouses—the others at Clark and Elm streets and Lincoln and Wrightwood avenues—in 1889 the company described the LaSalle Avenue and Illinois Street powerhouse as a "nest of machinery and power used for cable in the tunnel and the downtown loop, which is 12,500 feet long." Courtesy of North Chicago Street Railroad Company

Inset: From 1993 to 1999, as Michael Jordan's sports bar and restaurant, the former Cable Car Powerhouse sported a huge basketball on the roof of this landmarked, 1887 building. Courtesy of AP/Charles Bennett

But once cable cars went the way of horse-and-buggies, the three-story building's purpose changed with the times, housing an automobile shop—Loop Auto Service—through the early motoring days of the 1940s to mid-1960s. In 1967 it tapped into another, seemingly endless boom: restaurants. Ireland's, a popular seafood place, was first; later it was Lalo's; then Michael Jordan's; and (capitalizing on history) the Lasalle Power Company, a multi-level entertainment venue that closed in 2012. In 2013, another Chicago powerhouse moved in—Gino's East pizza. Swish.

NOW IT'S...

Was: North Chicago Street Railroad Company Cable Car Powerhouse

Is: Gino's East River North, Gino's Brewing Co., and the Comedy Bar

Location: 500 N LaSalle St.

Tip: The building's facade was moved seventeen feet west of its original location when LaSalle Street was widened in 1929.

Bubbly Battery Building

Pop the cork and celebrate the resurgence of the Carbide and Carbon building, transformed into a hotel.

Designed by Daniel Burnham's sons just before the Roaring 20s fell flat into the Great Depression, the distinctive green and gold color is said to have been chosen at an office party, influenced by the green glass and gold foil of a champagne bottle. In diary entries of meetings between Daniel Jr. and Union Carbide and Carbon Corp., Burnham wrote how much executives liked New York's American Radiator Building and the dark green color of a champagne bottle. They hoped the dramatic color would be a magnet for tenants' customers.

The $4.75 million green-tinted terra cotta and black granite building did stand out from the city's traditional skyscrapers. Architectural historian Carl Condit later wrote it was "the first skyscraper in Chicago to make extensive use of external color contrasts."

Built for the inventors of the dry cell battery called Eveready—the company was later named Union Carbide—the beloved art deco tower became home to the Midwest regional headquarters of the New York-based firm in 1929.

The forty-story Michigan Avenue landmark's "stunningly intact gold-and-white elevator lobby" is original, but the exterior didn't age well. In 1999, three years after developers discarded a plan to turn the building into two hundred condominiums, a pedestrian was hit by falling terra cotta.

The new owners safety-netted the building, then spent $106 million replacing, among other things, 7,700 matching green terra cotta blocks and much of the gold leaf. The gold has always been real twenty-four-karat on the edges and top three stories—1/5000 of an inch thick. Imitation decorative gold-colored sheeting was considered, and rejected, during the restoration.

Blair Kamin (2004): "A match made in architectural heaven, pairing a distinctive building with a distinctive hotel, and … restoring the multicolored glory of a once-ragged landmark skyscraper."

A 1928 *Tribune* article was headlined: "Green 'Nd Gold Tower Newest for Boul Mich —Splash of Color to Brighten Skyline." The article noted "the entire basement will be used for automobile storage, with a capacity of forty cars." Courtesy of Joni Hirsch Blackman

Inset: As part of the 2004 renovation, two neighboring 1920s buildings were demolished to make room for a seven-story addition to house restaurants and ballrooms. The top of the building was the filming location for an opening shooting scene in Morgan Freeman's 2008 film, *Wanted*. Courtesy of Joni Hirsch Blackman

The 381-room Hard Rock opened, appropriately, on New Year's Eve, December 31, 2003. Champagne toast required.

NOW IT'S . . .

Was: The Carbide & Carbon Building, Hard Rock Hotel

Is: An independent hotel

Location: 230 N Michigan Ave.

Tip: At the Michigan Avenue entrance, notice "CC" in the window above the doors, and inside, on the bronze elevator doors.

11

"The People's Palace"

One of the most popular attractions in the city—dubbed "The People's Palace" by the press when it was built.

But in the late 1800s, construction was delayed while two groups sparred for the last parcel of the federal government's Fort Dearborn, required to be preserved for public use. The city's first public library or a new war memorial honoring Civil War veterans? Four battles fought in court ended in 1891 with this cease-fire: the building would be shared— entrance for the library to the south and for the Grand Army of the Republic Rotunda and Memorial Hall on the north.

Plans were quite grand because the library board wanted the building to "convey . . . the idea that it is an enduring monument worthy of a great and public-spirited city." A library full of words can't express the extent to which they succeeded.

Designed by Art Institute's architects, the seventy-two-thousand-ton building rests on more than 2,300 oak-log piles, the first time deep-driven piles were ever used. Designed to prove the muddy young city was sophisticated, only the highest quality materials were used: rare imported marble, Favrile glass mosaics (which seem to sparkle everywhere), polished brass, fine hardwoods.

Hard surfaces were practical, too—easier to keep clean when you've got soot-filled Illinois Central railroad trains chugging along across the street (now covered by Millennium Park, a great view of which is possible from the center's Eastside windows.)

Opening in 1897, the city's first public library was filled with twelve thousand books sent from Britain after the Great Chicago Fire of 1871. The grand staircase leads to the former library's main circulation room, now the breathtaking Preston Bradley Hall capped by the world's largest stained-glass Tiffany Dome that was restored in 2008. This room? Truly a don't-miss.

Since 1991, this five-story building that looks like three has housed the nation's first and most comprehensive free municipal cultural venue—an arts showcase offering hundreds of free events yearly.

Designed by Shepley, Rutan & Coolidge, the first Chicago Public Library's entrances are on the side streets. Courtesy of Library of Congress

Inset: Civil War battle names are carved above the Memorial Hall doors; love of learning quotes in ten languages on two sides of the room. When entering the building on the library side, look up to the arch above that lists authors' names. Courtesy of Joni Hirsch Blackman

When a new library was needed in the 1960s, developers lined up for the Michigan Avenue property. Thankfully, the 1839 U.S. War Department document had the final word: the property can be used only for public purposes.

Again and decisively: the People's Palace.

NOW IT'S...

Was: Chicago Public Library

Is: Chicago Cultural Center - free music, dance and theater events, films, lectures, and art exhibitions.

Location: 78 E Washington St.

Tip: Ten marriage/civil union ceremonies are performed by judges at the Cultural Center one Saturday morning a month, by appointment only.

Holy Post Office, Batman!

Blame it on Chicago's huge twentieth century mail order businesses—Wards, Sears, Spiegel, and others. Catalogs and merchandise went through this post office to every state. As construction of the new facility was debated in 1915, Chicago Plan Commission chair Charles Wacker said, "The tremendous growth of the parcels post business must be reckoned with. . . . The fact that the parcels post business of Chicago already exceeds that of any other five cities of the country combined should be remembered. . . ."

By 1932's cornerstone-laying, Chicago boasted the world's largest post office building. The 2.5 million square feet of space originated with 1921's brick-sided Van Buren Street "parcel post center"; four towers and a lobby were added, opened in 1934, with Alabama marble and mosaic tiles on the walls.

The original sketches had one small problem: a future Congress Parkway extension to the west was called for in the 1909 Plan of Chicago and they didn't want the building—already constructed over tracks of four railroad companies—to stand in the way.

Holy design solution! (Two Batman movies were filmed at this building.) A hole at the base of the building was much appreciated twenty years later when the highway was constructed. A post office official noted in 1930, "an archway through the building to accommodate Congress Street would not complicate the building of the structure."

Decades of stamp increases later, the postal service in 1996 called the place "antiquated" and left. Redevelopment plans for the zoned-for-ten-million-square-feet site were many, varied, and undelivered for

Chicago's post office "was designed to facilitate movement of information on a broad and unprecedented scale . . . the primary mail distribution center of America," according to its National Register of Historic Places nomination.

In 1930, architect Ernest Graham noted the "herculean task" of designing a massive structure over working railroad tracks and with space for a future roadway. Courtesy of Curt Teich & Co.

Inset: The once-busy central post office's Art Deco lobby was resplendent with cream-colored marble and tile. Courtesy of Urban Remains

twenty years: no micro-apartments, no urban mall and entertainment complex, no casino, and no skyscraper. Meanwhile, the former gilded Art Deco masterpiece turned into an eyesore, with exterior broken stone and windows, plus interior decay after years of neglect and a couple of fires. The mayor threatened eminent domain.

But neither icy forecasts nor wet blankets nor dark economic weather could keep this post office from delivering—a sealed office-building deal in 2016 promised restoration of the exterior limestone and historic lobby with Bruce Wayne-worthy views.

NOW IT'S...

Was: Chicago Central Post Office

Is: Office Building

Location: 433 W Van Buren St.

Tip: Chicago's "western front door" with riverfront plaza/riverwalk and three-acre rooftop park is scheduled to open 2018-2020.

Building Now Sports Hotel Rooms

In January of 1891, the Chicago athletic club's 1,400 members announced plans for a new ten-story clubhouse on Michigan Avenue with "a bicycle track, running track, a restaurant, bowling alleys, shooting gallery, etc." The gymnasium would be two stories high: "the largest and best equipped athletic clubhouse in the United States," costing $500,000. It also included a barber shop, Turkish and Russian baths, twenty-six-table billiard room, small apartments, library, locker rooms, dressing rooms, private event rooms, racquet courts, tennis court, and a swimming "tank" (now an event space with a floor that looks like swim lanes).

Membership was capped at 2,000; annual dues ranged from $20-$40 with a $100 initiation fee. The wealthiest men in Chicago—Marshall Field, Cyrus McCormick, and A.G. Spaulding (co-founder of the National League baseball division)—were members of the athletic, business, and social club. Women? Not so much. They were allowed only for Wednesday dinners and Sunday afternoon concerts. It wasn't until 1972, 100 years after CAA's founding, the doors opened to women members.

The Venetian Gothic structure was designed by Henry Ives Cobb, who also designed much of the University of Chicago. It was completed during the summer of 1893 in time to impress visitors to the World's Fair.

"One of the most striking buildings in the country" closed in 2007 because of lagging membership. Sold to developers who planned to convert just a third of it into a hotel, the financial downturn upended that plan, leaving the building vacant for five years.

Sold again in 2012 to John Pritzker, son of the Hyatt Hotels co-founder, it was meticulously restored, featuring the iconic Cherry Circle Room restaurant; a bar/game room with bocce, pool, checkers/chess and

Logo in the billiards room look familiar? Chicago Athletic Association member William Wrigley appropriated the CAA red C on blue ground for his Cubs baseball team in the 1930s.

A 1905 photo of the Henry Ives Cobb-designed club. The double-tall, diamond-cut windows at the fourth and fifth floors were the original gymnasium, which had a running track on a fifth-floor balcony. Courtesy of Library of Congress

Inset: In 1891 and 1892, newspaper articles noted the eighth-floor balcony's size ("large enough to set tables and chairs upon for those who want to enjoy the fresh air") and exceptional location to enjoy "the magnificent view across Lake Michigan. Courtesy of Joni Hirsch Blackman

foosball; and a former speakeasy used by members during Prohibition—the eight-seat Milk Room micro-bar featuring vintage spirits.

With interiors in the hands of former Hollywood movie set designers, CAA opened in 2015 to rave reviews for its retro clubby and pure Chicago fun atmosphere—membership no longer needed.

NOW IT'S...

Was: Chicago Athletic Association Clubhouse

Is: Chicago Athletic Association Hotel

Location: 12 S Michigan Ave. and 71 E Madison St.

Tip: Cindy's, the popular rooftop bar/restaurant with a view of Millennium Park/Lake Michigan, is named after developer Pritzker's mother.

Read All About It

Unbiased journalism was innovative when Melville E. Stone founded the *Chicago Daily News* in 1875, promising it would be "independent of any political party" with "no axes to grind, no friends to reward, no enemies to punish." Its goal was "accuracy and impartiality" without sensational or scandalous material "for the purpose of making sales." All that for just one penny!

John Holabird once said the building he designed in 1929 exemplified the modern movement in American architecture, now known as Art Deco—quite different from the *Tribune*'s four-year-old neo-Gothic structure across town.

The first Chicago office building with a public plaza, it has a distinct Egyptian influence, resembling a Cubist sphinx. It's also the first significant commercial building to face the Chicago River and the first building to be built on air rights over railroad tracks. Smoke from the steam locomotives was drawn up like a chimney by fans into smokestacks through the twenty-six stories of the building and vented out the top.

The newspaper's press room took up the first three floors, offices for the paper were the next four. The Daily News's WMAQ radio station was housed on the top two floors.

In 1960, Marshall Field IV bought the paper that had won thirteen Pulitzer prizes and moved it to the Sun-Times Building on Wabash Avenue at the river. The former Daily News Building was renamed Two North Riverside Plaza, while its previous tenant, the afternoon paper, began a slow decline coinciding with the rise of television news. *The Daily News* ceased publication after March 4, 1978.

At the start of the new millennium, Two North Riverside Plaza was threatened with being razed and replaced or converted to condominiums. But unlike its first tenant, it survived, was renovated in 2010, and is still newsworthy.

The city's second most-popular paper after the *Chicago Tribune* was published each afternoon. One of the first with foreign bureaus, the *Daily News* also pioneered classified ads and comics syndication.

The newspaper's press room took up the first three floors; offices for the paper were the next four. WMAQ radio station was housed on the top two floors; the Chicago & North Western Railway and other businesses leased floors in between. Courtesy of Curt Teich Co.

Inset: The original plaza fountain, long a makeshift planter, will soon be restored. Through the doors under the bronze south transom one finds a hallway lined with shops and food offerings amid silver Art Deco detailing. Courtesy of Joni Hirsch Blackman

NOW IT'S ...

Was: Chicago Daily News Building

Is: Two North Riverside Plaza

Location: 2 N Riverside; 400 W Madison

Tip: Bas-relief panels on the public plaza along the river honor journalists such as owner, editor, and plaza namesake Victor Lawson.

King Arthur Danced Here

It looks like a castle, is as large as a castle, and—go figure—for a while it actually was called "Castle," but the huge 1892 Romanesque Revival structure designed by Henry Ives Cobb was actually built as the replacement home for the Chicago Historical Society because its first building had been destroyed in the Great Chicago Fire of 1871.

Now known as the Chicago History Museum, the society moved to Lincoln Park in 1931, leaving the massive landmark at Dearborn and Ontario to house a line of successors: a magazine publisher, the Works Progress Administration, the Loyal Order of Moose, the Chicago Institute of Design, and various recording studios (1950s and 1960s). Empty for a while in the late 1970s, it was transformed in 1985 into The Limelight nightclub, a multi-floor "mega-bar."

Four years later, after a year-long, multi-million-dollar remodeling (adding 17,000 square feet to the original 30,000) it re-opened as Excalibur. Its twenty-four-year reign as Chicago's largest nightclub featured various sub-venues such as the Cabaret, "Club X" dance club, Vision, The Dome Room, and high-energy "barcades." Excalibur—one of an elite group of clubs to earn the term "legendary"—hosted the official Chicago Bulls Championship parties during each of the "three-peat" years, 1991-1993 and 1996-1998.

Re-named Castle in 2013, the new sound system was recognized as the "best in the world" in 2014. But an offer Ala Carte Entertainment couldn't refuse ($12 million) closed the nightclub in January 2015. The purchase by Four Corners Tavern Group left the building temporarily closed. No word yet whether the ghosts long rumored to haunt the building—featured on the Travel Channel's *Ghost Adventurers* in 2012—are staying on.

Excalibur's beer cooler on the top floor featured two miles of beer lines that fed all eleven bars from an eight-hundred-square-foot refrigerated room.

Known as the Gallery Club in January 1972, burglars forced open a rear door and used sledge hammers to open a walk-in safe. Courtesy of Library of Congress

Inset: In 1999, Prince visited the Excalibur and gave an unscheduled concert in the main club. He showed up several more times, giving short "pop-up" performances occasionally, such as in 2001 after a gig at Lincoln Park's Park West. Courtesy of Joni Hirsch Blackman

NOW IT'S ...

Was: Chicago Historical Society

Is: Future Four Corners Tavern/Nightclub

Location: 632 N Dearborn St.

Tip: A nightclub called "The Factory"—proposed in 1969 by several celebrities, including Sammy Davis Jr. and Paul Newman—never materialized.

Art Deco Architecture and Autos

Just try finding another Hampton Inn in a building like this one. Once called "the most beautiful building in America," superlatives continue to describe the transformation of the former Wacker Tower into a 143-room hotel whose refurbishment has recaptured its best features (for a mere $41 million).

Despite speedy construction of the smallish skyscraper—just 265 days of 1928; opening January 1929—the seventeen-story building is considered one of Chicago's finest Art Deco skyscrapers. Designed by Holabird & Roche, the iconic architectural firm changed its name mid-project to Holabird & Root after the death of Martin Roche.

Originally the headquarters of the Chicago Motor Club—founded to improve roads, provide emergency assistance and offer route information to increasing numbers of drivers— it's hard to tell who loves this place more: architecture or auto geeks. But anyone who remembers "TripTiks" should go.

Those narrow, custom-bound pages of maps highlighting routes for trip-taking, including points of interest and other travel advice, were dispensed from this lobby during those pre-GPS years. The old TripTik counters have been replaced by a bar, but the fabulously stylized Art Deco map of cross country routes by muralist John Warner Norton remains above the elevators. The twenty-nine-foot-wide non-foldable U.S. map is restored, resplendent in a blast-from-the-past reminder of the days when driving cross-country was a visceral adventure along old routes such as the Lincoln and Dixie Highways.

The Motor Club moved to Des Plaines in 1986. Purchased with an eye toward condo conversion, rental office tenants remained until 2004. Brakes were applied to 2006 talk of sending this sputtering classic to the scrap heap—partially thanks to its somewhat tiny site that wouldn't have attracted much attention for a teardown.

Described as the "temple of transport" and "monument to the progress of motordom" in 1929; A "love song to the freedom to travel around the country in your car" in 2015.

The business of the motor club—TripTix and other services—was conducted from the desks at the right of Holabird & Root's Art Deco lobby. Courtesy of The Art Institute of Chicago

Inset: The Chicago Motor Club's Art Deco building opened on Jan. 27, 1929. Courtesy of The Art Institute of Chicago

Finally, landmarked by the city in 2012, it opened as a Hampton Inn (with road-themed room signs) on May 19, 2015—the Motor Club's Art Deco "C" intertwined with a red star on the doorway, roaring back across the finish line.

NOW IT'S...

Was: The Chicago Motor Club

Is: Hampton Inn Downtown/North Loop/Michigan Avenue

Location: 68 E Wacker Place

Tip: A 1928 Ford Model A is parked on a balcony at the lobby's far end, holding court where cars once ruled.

A Lot of Bones about the Park

The bones of the story were known, but details were unearthed, so to speak, by Northwestern art theory lecturer/photographer Pamela Bannos. Now the foremost expert on the fifty-seven-acre City Cemetery on the southern edge of what's now Lincoln Park (northeast of Clark Street and North Avenue), Bannos believes as many as a third of the thirty-five-thousand bodies once buried there remain.

Part of the large land tract given to Illinois by the Federal Government in 1837 was designated a cemetery; burials began in 1843. As the years (and graves, particularly after 1849's cholera epidemic) went on, the cemetery expanded north, to about Armitage. More than two hundred victims of 1854's cholera epidemic were buried in the large anonymous graveyard for the poor, Potter's Field, on the eastern edge where baseball fields are now located.

Only 1858's large tomb of millionaire Ira Couch is left from the cemetery because it was thought too expensive to remove. Concerns about the cemetery's deteriorating condition were noted that year, three years after a newspaper suggestion to turn the prime property into a park.

In 1859, Dr. John Rauch, later Illinois Board of Health president, lobbied for the cemetery's closure, believing corpses located below the water table could send bacteria into the lake, aka the city's water supply. Lot sales were suspended as Rosehill Cemetery opened in Lake View, on higher ground several miles north of the city limits. Burials continued in previously-sold lots until 1866 and in Potter's Field, where four thousand Civil War rebels who died at Camp Douglas were interred between 1862-65.

After President Abraham Lincoln's assassination in April 1865, Lake Park (the sixty acres north of the cemetery formerly known as Cemetery

The Great Chicago Fire "burned markers, a lot of which were wood ... the flames cracked and charred and broke marble headstones ... If there's no marker, you don't know what's there." (Bannos)

This 1863 plat map is laid over a recent NASA/Google Satellite map of Lincoln Park. It was created by Pamela Bannos, an artist who researched the story of "Chicago Cemetery, subsequently known as the City Cemetery, then the Old Cemetery, then Lincoln Park," whose work was also the source for the entry. Courtesy of Pamela Bannos

Park), was renamed Lincoln Park. Graves were supposedly moved to other cemeteries during the next twenty years, but that slow process was hampered by the Great Chicago Fire of 1871, which desecrated many markers.

Officials reported the last of the bodies were removed in 1887. But human bones are found nearly any time shovels disturb parkland—rows of coffins in 1899, a skeleton and casket while digging the zoo barn foundation in 1962, and remains of eighty-one people when constructing the museum's parking garage in 1998.

NOW IT'S...

Was: Chicago Cemetery/City Cemetery

Is: Lincoln Park

Location: 500-5700 N Lake Shore Dr.

Tip: Bannos' website, hiddentruths.northwestern.edu is "the most thorough exploration of the cemetery's history," said the Chicago History Museum's chief historian.

Opera's Clothes Hung Here

In October 1925, the Chicago Civic Opera was anticipating a song-filled future in the massive forty-two-story architectural gem under construction along the Chicago River (which was completed in 1929.) Meanwhile, supporting players were moving into a brand-new $550,000 studio/warehouse built several miles to the south for the manufacture and care for "all of the accoutrements of opera," according to the *Chicago Tribune*.

More than 1,500 truckloads of items from 100-plus operas that had previously been stored in two leased warehouses were moved to the new five-story warehouse/workshop/garage.

One of few in the country specifically built to store and create opera sets, props, and stages, the warehouse contained the "largest and finest scenic studio in the world" where sketches of settings were drawn. It housed a steam laundry to clean costumes; a carpentry shop filled with power saws, lathes, and wood-carving tools; a room of foot-high opera stage models for planning scenery and lighting; and "electrically-driven sewing machines" for making costumes.

In 1958, when the five-year-old Lyric Opera took it over, a *Tribune* reporter viewed scenery stacked up to thirty feet high; models of period furniture and a spinning wheel hanging from string looped around pipes—props and scenery that would have cost $10 million to replace, including some nearly fifty-year-old items from when Chicago's first opera company opened in 1910.

Another half-century later, in 2004, the Lyric held a clearance sale before vacating the one-hundred-thousand-square-foot building for another new warehouse. For sale were hundreds of trunks full of thousands of costumes—some a century old with "Property of Chicago Civic Opera"

"Every working day in the year the warehouse is in operation, for the building of properties, scenery, armor, wigs, costumes, and electrical apparatus," business manager Herbert M. Johnson explained in the mid-1900s.

A 1926 view of the 100,000-square-foot warehouse that also included a truck garage to move scenery back to the Opera House. Courtesy of Chicago History Museum

Inset: Some pre-moving sale items decorate the front door and the corner of the Opera Lofts building. Courtesy of Joni Hirsch Blackman

tags still sewn inside—a papier-mâchée swan, parasols, a nine-foot-long red velvet sofa on wheels, a throne, faux-grandfather clocks, and a gargoyle.

The old warehouse became ninety-three residential units in 2008. The lofts feature a green roof with a dog run—phrases likely never uttered back in 1925, even in song.

NOW IT'S...

Was: Chicago Civic Opera warehouse

Is: Opera Lofts

Location: 2545 S Dearborn St.

Tip: Items purchased from the clearance sale were incorporated into the Opera Lofts common areas and a statue hangs from the building's corner.

School of Talk . . . and Talkies

Named after the upcoming Columbian Exposition, the Columbia School of Oratory was founded in 1890. Advertising in the local newspapers described a private institution teaching elocution, oratory, and physical culture.

The name changed to Columbia College of Expression in 1905. Partnering with the Pestalozzi Froebel Teachers' College in 1927, the schools moved from their former locations, renting the seventh floor of 618 S Michigan Ave. (The schools separated in 1944, about the same time Columbia added television, journalism, advertising, and business to its radio, theater, and drama curricula.) The Arcade Building's classes were held on the seventh floor until 1936, but in the 1950s, it became the Midwestern Regional offices of IBM Corp.

In 1974 (the same year Columbia College was awarded accreditation from the North Central Association of Colleges and Schools) 618 S Michigan became The Spertus Institute until 2006, when the growing Columbia College Chicago returned, purchasing its previously rented home.

Columbia had purchased its first building at 600 S Michigan Ave. thirty years earlier, permanently settling in the South Loop. Now Alexandroff Campus Center, the brick building with its Art Deco lobby was constructed for the International Harvester Company in 1906.

Other Columbia buildings:

Getz Theater, 72 E 11th St., architect Holabird & Root, 1927-30—The Chicago Women's Club hosted rallies to support women's voting rights.

Music Department, 1014 S Michigan Ave., Christian Eckstrom, 1912—Built for a shingle distributor, it was renovated in 1941 to become the Sherwood Conservatory of Music, where Phyllis Diller was a piano student.

Dance Center, 1306 S Michigan Ave., Anker S. Graven, 1929—A film exchange for 1930s independent cinema operators called Paramount Public Corp.

Kick high when passing 624 S Michigan Ave. Ziegfield Follies' producer Flo Ziegfield Jr.'s father, Florenz, was involved in the building's original purpose—Chicago Musical College.

Chicago Musical College was later the Blum, Grant Park, Barnheisel, and Torco buildings. Courtesy of Columbia College of Chicago

Inset: The short building behind the trolley had been a 1920s nightclub, a restaurant, a textile company and Universal Bowling Corp.'s salesroom. Courtesy of Columbia College Chicago

Wabash Campus, 623 S Wabash Ave., Alfred Alschuler, 1925—The Studebaker Brothers' Carriage Company's regional office/warehouse. Later owned by the Brunswick Co.

Theater/Film Annex, 1415 S Wabash Ave., unknown architect—A Hudson-Ross store in the 1950s, a garage/service station in the 1970s.

916 & 1000 S Wabash, unknown architect—Belonged to the Chicago Housing Authority until 2007. Previously a garage and the American Wholesale Furniture Company.

NOW IT'S...

Is: Columbia College Chicago

Tip: The college's original philosophies of "Theory never made an artist" and "learn to do by doing" are concepts still in practice at Columbia.

Burnham's Last Bank

Famed Chicago Architect Daniel Burnham had already decided to make this his last business architecture design. He planned to "devote his entire time to the work of beautifying cities, a work in which he was vitally interested," a June 4, 1912, *Chicago Tribune* article noted. Ironically, it turned out to be the last structure he designed before his death.

The $6 million bank completed in 1914 was one of the largest office buildings in the world and the first private building to occupy an entire Chicago block—bounded by LaSalle, Adams, Quincy Streets, and "Fifth Avenue," now Wells Street. Forty-five-feet-tall columns facing LaSalle Street were the largest columns in the city—Doric, complementing the Ionic and Corinthian columns of its immediate neighbors.

The banking floor, nearly as large as a football field, was the largest in the world, unusual in that it was a large central bank of three associated banks—banks that would, according to a 1923 bank history, "give Chicago and the West the banking services they required."

The planned height of the building was a concern, because on Sept. 1, 1911, the city's new restriction of 200 feet would go into effect. Burnham's design called for 260 feet toward the sky.

"No one else can work out and determine the final plan and delegation, and I must stick to it day and night until this is accomplished," he wrote, two weeks before the deadline.

The monumental structure features a first-floor grand marble staircase leading to the second-floor banking hall. Burnham believed office buildings should be "monuments to commerce" the way ornate libraries and government offices honored public institutions.

Over the years, the office building had deteriorated until it was purchased in 2005 with thoughts of upgrading. But the success of a nearby luxury hotel prompted consideration of how well this building's large floor plates would fit that booming industry.

"May be regarded as the culmination of the important work done in the last fifteen years of the firm of D.H. Burnham and Company," *The Architectural Record*, July 1915.

The twenty-one-story building replaced the razed Rand-McNally office building, the first steel skyscraper the famed architect had designed. Courtesy of V. O. Hammon Publishing Co.

Inset: Later Continental Illinois Bank and Trust, the building is constructed around a large open light court that can be seen from the Willis Tower Skydeck. Courtesy of JW Marriott

The $396 million renovation into a twelve-floor, JW Marriott was completed in 2010. Two large ballrooms were created out of the former three-story, barrel-vaulted banking hall—on the money for the original "make no small plans" architect.

NOW IT'S...

Was: Continental and Commercial National Bank Building

Is: JW Marriott Chicago

Location: 208 S LaSalle St. and 151 W Adams St.

Tip: The lobby allows public passage from LaSalle Street to Wells Street—check out the Burnham Ballroom with its original domed ceiling.

Murderers, Bootleggers, Gamblers, and Anarchists

History permeates this place—the two previous structures on the land were infamous, the current building was the site of famous trials, and its veteran courthouse reporters the premise for a play.

Before it was built, countless newspaper stories detailed arguments justifying the previous courthouse's future. In December 1890, a Grand Jury pronounced the old building "totally unfitted for the purpose for which it is now used. With the World's Fair coming . . . in 1893, we ought to have the finest court building in the world to show our visitors."

The finest is what they got—a courthouse so iconic in its solid Romanesque style, it was imitated by courthouses built throughout the Northeast, Midwest, and Southeast for the next two decades.

The ten-courtroom, six-story Bedford limestone structure features an arched entrance on which relief sculptures of women representing law and justice rest. It served as the county courthouse through 1929—a year after *The Front Page* was written by two newspapermen, Ben Hecht and Charles MacArthur, who had worked in that fourth-floor pressroom for years.

Those years were filled with cases both routine and scandalous, including the 1921 trial involving eight members of the so-called "Black Sox" (in what is now called the "Shoeless Joe" courtroom after the most famous banned-from-baseball White Sox player), and the 1924 trial of accused murderers, University of Chicago students Leopold and Loeb. Al Capone, Chicago's most notorious bootlegger, was often brought there for questioning but never for trial.

For ten years, the building stood vacant before housing various other city and county agencies until 1985, when the deteriorating building was sold to a group of developers led by Albert Friedman (former member, one-time chair, of the city's Landmarks Commission).

After listing notorious criminals tried at the old Criminal Courts building, the *Tribune's* May 1893 headline described the new "Citadel of Justice—No Structure of Like Nature Anywhere to Equal It."

Architect Otto Matz designed a "monumental edifice with powerful massing" according to its landmark nomination a century after its 1893 construction. Courtesy of Friedman Properties

Inset: Bordering the courthouse's arched doorway are two carved figures—two reclining females—one carrying a book signifying law and the other with a sword representing justice. Courtesy of Library of Congress

After witnessing a painstaking restoration, Alderman Bernard Stone was quoted by the *Tribune*: "The old Criminal Courts Building is about as much an historical landmark as anything could possibly be. And how!"

NOW IT'S ...

Was: Cook County Criminal Courts Building

Is: Courthouse Place office building

Location: 54 W Hubbard St.

Tip: North Market Hall was built here in 1851; when the Hall went up in smoke in 1872, it was replaced by the first Criminal Court and County Jail.

Wish You Were Here!

Curt Teich (pronounced "tike") kept fifteen copies of every postcard his printing company produced from 1898-1974—a collection of images from one hundred thousand towns and cities throughout the world. Some one thousand employees working three shifts produced millions of postcards each day during the peak years.

Teich, an immigrant whose father operated a newspaper chain in Germany, opened a downtown printshop in 1898 until a client suggested he specialize. The first picture postcard (no envelope required) had been created for the 1893 World's Fair. When 1898 postal regulations created a penny stamp for them, specializing in the new photographic "media" was a turn-of-the-century no-brainer.

Traveling across the country via train in 1905, Teich stopped in countless small towns and took photos for the postcards himself. Later, when salespeople/photographers were added, they expanded to seventy-five other countries.

In 1910, Teich moved to a seventeen-year-old factory on the north side of town that became the largest volume postcard printer in the world, employing more than one hundred artists to retouch the photos.

Postcards featured roadside attractions, architecture, famous highways such as Route 66, and even interiors of buildings. The company inadvertently created an invaluable historical record of twentieth century Americana from fashion to transportation, and items in the 320,000-plus collection are often sought after by magazines such as *Vogue* and *Rolling Stone*. Ralph Teich donated the collection to the Lake County Museum in 1982; they gave it to Chicago's Newberry Library in 2016.

During World War II, the company produced about half of all maps used by U.S. troops, ceding its postcard printing lead forever. But the retro postcards keep the Teich name—and nostalgia—alive.

A large safe was discovered while renovating the factory. Too big to remove—it was as big as a room!—the developers just converted it into a (large) closet.

A Curtis Teich postcard of the Curtis Teich Postcard Company. Courtesy of Curt Teich & Co.

Inset: Now Postcard Place lofts, the letters C T are still clearly carved in medallions on the top of each corner of the doorway marked with a yellow awning. Courtesy of Joni Hirsch Blackman

NOW IT'S ...

Was: Curt Teich Co. Postcard Printing

Is: Postcard Place Lofts

Location: 1733 W Irving Park Rd.

Tip: Converted to lofts in 1990, various floors in the (private) former factory display Curt Teich postcards and old printing photo blocks.

Thriving, Even Without Roof and Train Shed

Downtown Chicago once boasted six railroad terminals, including 1885's Dearborn Street Station at Dearborn and Polk Streets, which remains one of the oldest railroad stations in the United States.

The station's several steeply pitched roofs were later removed, but the twelve-story tall clock tower that welcomed travelers remains a focal point. The station was expanded to accommodate the crush of visitors to the 1893 World's Columbian Exposition.

A 1922 fire destroyed the roof of the brick, terra cotta, and granite station but a third floor was added during reconstruction. As many as twenty-five railway lines, with 122 commuter and inter-city trains carrying 17,000 passengers, passed through the station daily in the 1920s, offering service to cities across the country—particularly the west—and into Canada. Freight trains served the printing houses in Printer's Row. The huge 165-by-700-foot train shed was one of the largest in the Midwest.

Trains going to and from Hollywood were common, carrying celebrities and business magnates to and through Chicago in luxurious private cars. From the 1920s through the '40s, it was the place to spot movie stars almost every day.

Passenger traffic remained high until the 1960s, but the commercial buildings emptied when printing companies left the area. In the 1970s and '80s, those buildings were converted into loft spaces and mixed retail. Passenger train travel, strongly affected by increases in expressway and airline travel, diminished. Ending in 1971, Amtrak consolidated downtown stations at Union Station, closing Dearborn and leaving it mostly empty for years.

In the early 1980s, Skidmore, Ownings & Merrill designed a master plan for one of the most successful urban renewal projects in the country at the time—Dearborn Park.

Cars are lined up waiting for passengers to disembark from trains—the old train shed can be seen behind the station. Courtesy of Curt Teich Co.

Demolition seemed imminent as at-grade tracks were removed and the train shed was torn down in 1976. Preservation-minded residents saved the "headhouse"—the building and clock tower—and it became the entry to the Dearborn Park residential development that rose on the former rail yard. The celebrities moved on, but Dearborn Station remains a star.

NOW IT'S...

Was: Dearborn Street Railroad Station

Is: The Dearborn Station, 120,000 square feet of retail and office space

Location: 47 W Polk St.

Tip: The city's oldest freestanding railroad station offers a lobby with chairs and tables for lingering ... or, even still, people-watching.

Freezer with Water out the Door

Milestones were racked up like ice cubes by this one-time gigantic freezer: The steel-frame building was described at construction in 1898 as resting on Norway piles driven to hard pan clay, "the longest ever driven in Chicago—fifty-five feet." When converted to residential use ninety years later, developers claimed that "no one has ever attempted conversion of a cold storage facility to residential use."

Equipped with "three high speed elevators and electric lights," 1898's description continued: "rolling steel doors opening on to the river, through which freight will be handled from the vessels, the building being so constructed that deeply laden boats can unload into the basement and light laden vessels on to the first floor." That is, more subzero than ice chest.

The cost? $300,000. The location? Apparently priceless: "One of the best for warehouse purposes in Chicago."

When leased in September 1898, "the Druecker warehouse (was) superior to most structures of the kind." Yet it was sold at foreclosure a year later, then sold to the North American Cold Storage company in 1904, just months before "an extensive addition to the already large plant" was constructed.

Fast-forward nearly seventy-five years: Architect Harry Weese's plan to convert the building to residences with developer Jack Wogan of Denver included two additional buildings with restaurants, office space, shops and a marina, collectively called "Wolf Point Landing."

Empty freezers need defrosting. Big freezer like this? Six months thawing time.

"The giant industrial ice box was constructed like a fortress. Matted horsehair originally insulated the windowless building and over the years it was followed by cork and then a foam material." Dec. 13, 1981 *Chicago Tribune.*

This is a 1910 view of the North American Cold Storage Warehouse, designed by Frank Abbott. This was one of the earliest steel and concrete structures built in downtown Chicago, according to the Art Institute. Courtesy of Art Institute of Chicago

Insulation had to be pried off walls with machines or chiseled off by hand. Miles of two-inch steel pipes that had circulated brine-and-ammonia refrigerant were cut out and disposed of.

At the 1979 renovation kick-off, plans remained. But soaring interest rates had cooled the once-hot condo market; by 1981, though newspapers called Fulton House "one of the most interesting and creative recycling jobs in the city," future phases went the way of the ice box.

NOW IT'S...

Was: Druecker Warehouse; North American Cold Storage building

Is: Fulton House condominiums

Location: 345 N Canal St.

Tip: Though Weese's longtime vision for a community on the river didn't materialize, he designed the next-door River Cottages.

A Snapshot in Time

Two camera-related things happened in Chicago in 1905: the Eastman Kodak Co. built a manufacturing facility and City Hall complained a photographer "plying his vocation whenever and wherever he pleases, making whomever he chooses his victim regardless of circumstances or surroundings, is becoming a general nuisance."

In January 1906, the city council passed an ordinance regulating "the evil of the Kodak fiend." The new law read: "[n]o person shall take photographs in the streets or public grounds of any person or persons without his or their consent." Penalties ranged from $10 to $100— eighteen years after George Eastman's Kodak camera, invented in 1888, was designed to "make photography accessible to the public!"

The company's local building received much less mention. A small item in April 1905 noted, "The New York Kodak company is now erecting a plant at the northeast corner of Eighteenth Street and Indiana Avenue, and altogether four or five factories have secured locations along that avenue within the last year or two."

Eastman Kodak expanded several times throughout the 1930s, purchasing several lots to the east.

The original building became Consolidated Book Publishers in the 1970s. In 1993, it became the first loft building in the Prairie Avenue area to convert to residential use, not unlike how Kodak was the first commercial loft in the formerly residential area. Prairie District lofts were a catalyst for the transformation of the South Loop. (Ironically, in 1981, it was said about the area: "Nobody lives around here.")

The Eastman Kodak building at first offered one hundred rental units to local artists, with monthly rents ranging from (hold onto your instamatics here . . .) $500 to $1,000 a month for 1,200 to 3,000 square

A bellows-type camera—popular in 1905 when the film/camera company built this building—is carved in the keystone above the 18th Street entrance of the former Eastman Kodak Company.

The Hill & Woltersdorf-designed Eastman Kodak plant, c. 1905, was constructed on South Indiana Avenue at a time when several other factories were also buying land there. Courtesy of Glessner House Museum

Inset: In 1992, the five-story, 190,000 square-foot brick Kodak building was converted to residential units, Prairie District Lofts. The camera sculpted in limestone sits above the south entrance. Courtesy of Joni Hirsch Blackman

feet of space. The five-story brick building later became condominiums. Meanwhile, one can only imagine what the 1906 City Council would want to do about cell phone cameras.

NOW IT'S...

Was: Eastman Kodak Co. Building

Is: Prairie District Lofts

Location: 1727 S Indiana Ave.

Tip: The lofts are across from the Prairie Avenue Historic District, near historic landmarks Glessner House and Clarke House.

Brick and Mortarboards

When E. R. Moore Company constructed its new brick factory at a cost of $16,000 in 1914, probably no one guessed the amount would be similar to a year of college tuition a century later.

Edwin R. Moore's cap, gown, and tassel manufacturing company supplied caps and gowns to DePaul University, its very first customer, in 1907. Each year, the firm outfitted graduations at seven thousand colleges, universities, high schools, junior highs, grade schools, even kindergartens. The firm produced thirty-four colors of caps and gowns, with royal blue the most popular for high schools, black for colleges.

Some of the more unusual clients were American University in Beirut, Lebanon, and McDonald's Hamburger University in Oak Brook. Caps and gowns were produced at a factory downstate, but tassels were woven at the Grace Street factory. Caps and gowns were also cleaned, repaired, and stored there, awaiting the next season's graduates. Officials noted that the company was the "seventh-largest dry cleaner in the world."

The company also provided gowns for clergy and judges, and in 1939 published a booklet by Helen Walters called, *The Story of Caps and Gowns*, which outlines everything you maybe never needed to know about ceremonial robes.

The second-largest cap and gown manufacturer in the U.S. for years, officials said while operating out of the Grace Street factory the company outfitted more than fifty million American students with Moore caps and gowns. The Moore family sold the business in the 1980s, and the Chicago factory closed in 2005.

The two connected buildings were converted into ninety-one condominiums in 2010—consider it a virtual moving of the tassel from one side to the other.

"Moore became interested in the academic costume field through Mrs. Moore's father, who had been engaged in this and kindred lines since 1878 ... " wrote Helen Waters in 1939.

At ER Moore in 1962, tassels were sorted at the plant according to their colors, later moved to the cap assembly area, May 5, 1962. Courtesy of UPI

Inset: The Lofts at 1800 complex consists of two buildings with a courtyard in between. Courtesy of Joni Hirsch Blackman

NOW IT'S...

Was: E. R. Moore Company Cap & Gown factory

Is: The Lofts at 1800

Location: 1800 W Grace St.

Tip: The country's first high school to graduate in caps and gowns instead of suits and dresses? Chicago's Englewood High, Class of 1911.

Hollywood's Chicago Location

Early 1900s movie-making meant Chicago, not Hollywood. Founded in 1907 as the Peerless Film Manufacturing Co. in what's now Old Town, it moved in 1909 to Uptown with the new name it took later in 1907, a combination of the founders' surname initials—Spoor and Anderson. The first film, *An Awful Skate*, was likely the only time a movie's star was also the studio janitor, Ben Turpin.

From 1907 to 1918, Essanay was one of the biggest film studios in the world, launching the silent movie careers of Gloria Swanson and Wallace Beery, and rocketing comic Charlie Chaplin to worldwide fame. Chaplin's 1915 film, *His New Job*, was one of some 1,500 films made in Chicago at the staggering rate of six movies a week.

George Spoor, a Waukegan Opera House manager from 1896 to 1898, was the first 35 mm projector distributor. Kinodrome Service provided his projector, films, and an operator to movie theaters nationwide. An employee, Donald Bell, joined with Albert Howell in 1907 to start their own movie projector company—Bell & Howell.

Historians call Essanay "the MGM of the silents." Few of those movies survive, but they include Essanay's 1916 *Sherlock Holmes*, a popular movie about the famous gumshoe.

Anderson, who later was worldwide cowboy star Broncho Billy in many short silent films, brought the studio's newest star to Chicago in 1914. English comic Charles Spencer Chaplin briefly stayed (23 days!) in Chicago, then made films at Essanay's California studio, including *The Tramp*. Chaplin switched studios in 1916, leaving Essanay reeling just as the film industry was shifting westward.

"Essanay was important in turning moviemaking into a well-organized industry," cultural historian Tim Samuelson told the *Tribune*. "They made films and found an efficient way to distribute them ... they were pioneers."

"It was one of the top studios of its time," said David Kiehn, a film historian based in Niles, California, where Essanay had its West Coast studios. "The majority of their films came out of Chicago, so these buildings have great historical value." Courtesy of Niles Essanay Silent Film Museum

Inset: The Essanay doorway along Argyle Street; the Terra Cotta heads of two Indians, the studio's trademark. A painting of Charlie Chaplin has been painted on a wall to the right as cars exit the parking lot. Courtesy of Joni Hirsch Blackman

The Argyle Street building was sold in 1932 to Wilding Pictures. In 1973, it was given to non-profit WTTW-TV, which used it through the late 1970s; other former tenants include Technicolor's Midwest office. St. Augustine College bought the building when the school was founded in 1980. The former "sound" stage where sophisticated indoor lighting was pioneered, now Charlie Chaplin Auditorium, is utilized often by the college. The original catwalk and lighting grid structures remain, as do Essanay's basement vaults . . . and a certain bygone aura.

NOW IT'S . . .

Was: Essanay Film Manufacturing Co.

Is: St. Augustine College's Charlie Chaplin Auditorium

Location: 1333-45 W Argyle St.

Tip: No formal tours are offered, but visitors may ask to look at the auditorium whenever the college offices are open.

Great Chicago Firehouse

Horses were still pulling fire equipment when the city's oldest existing firehouse was built, just two years after the Great Chicago Fire. The two-story, two-bay firehouse opened on July 1, 1873, in a Maxwell Street neighborhood populated with immigrants. Engine Co. 18 made more fire runs than any other house—six hundred a year.

The old stable was eventually turned into a dining room. While a kitchen was installed where the hay had been stored, the hole in the wall where hay was thrown to the horses remained. Indeed, not much has changed in the small station, where the floor has been supported by six-by-six wooden posts in the basement, for more than 130 years.

"We've replaced the two-thousand-pound horse with a forty-thousand-pound truck," Fire Commissioner James Joyce said in announcing the house would be retired in 2008. "Something has to give, and that house is showing its age."

Engine 18 moved to a brand-new, single-level station. The old station was sold for $320,000 two years later and converted into a firehouse of a different sort: for ceramics and glassblowing. The Firehouse Art Studio has kept as much of the original detail as possible, including the original wooden staircase, metal fire poles and the small room where fire hoses used to be stored.

The art and community center offers affordable programs—focusing on fire-based art forms—for all ages.

""We think it's a really great idea with a cool name that incorporates the history of the building," a city spokeswoman told the *Tribune*. "No one's going to forget it was a firehouse."

Between the red doors and the "City of Chicago Fire Department" carved above the door—not a fireball's chance in water.

Engine 18 moved in 2008 to 1360 S Blue Island Ave., which is famously known as "House 51," featured on the NBC-TV show *Chicago Fire*—there, visitors are welcome!

Undated photo of Engine Co. 18, the first Chicago Fire Department company organized after the Fire of 1871. It occupied a temporary wooden frame firehouse in December 1872, then moved to this brick firehouse on July 1, 1873. Courtesy of The Firehouse Art Studio

Inset: Engine Co. 18 moved in 2008. Jay Nowak and Jessica Beauchemin bought the 7,500-square-foot building, renovating it into the Firehouse Art Studio, where fire-based art forms that need to be treated at extremely high temperatures are right at home. Courtesy of The Firehouse Art Studio

NOW IT'S...

Was: Chicago Fire Station, Engine Co. 18

Is: Fire House Art Studio

Location: 1123 W Roosevelt Rd.

Tip: Across the street sit two pre-Chicago Fire landmarks—Holy Family Church (1857) and St. Ignatius College Prep (1869).

Heavenly Circus Training

Whatever praying is going on in this building that still looks like a church, it is probably something like "Please let me catch that trapeze!"

Trapeze artists, tightrope walkers, and other aerial acrobats are flying through the heavenly space built in 1907, featuring stained glass windows and a bell tower. When the church was put up for sale, many expected the Logan Square property would be turned into condominiums. Then Aloft Circus Arts owner Shayna Swanson saw the building (with its adjacent two-flat of three apartments) online.

"I first walked in, I started crying," Swanson said. "I was like, 'This is it!'"

The former First Evangelical Church was such a perfect fit that the exterior and much of the interior remained virtually untouched as it transformed into an inspiring training space. Pews were removed and rigging was installed across the church's almost-forty-foot-high wooden beams, and viola! An elite circus school.

Opened in 2016, student performers and amateur enthusiasts alike learn such things as trapeze, aerial skills, pole acrobatics, trampoline, tight-wire, hand-balancing, and clowning there.

Founded in 2005 and formerly located in West Town, Aloft is the third-largest circus school in the country, training students for productions like Cirque du Soleil in the six-thousand-square-foot former congregation area. In the bell-less former bell tower, aerial training happens twenty feet above the floor, and a small, easily-heated room on the main level is home to contortion training.

The church's balcony was chosen for a "tramp wall"—a circus act where performers bounce off a trampoline and run up and off walls. Already the region's premiere circus learning and training center, Swanson's high-flying hopes include that the building will become the world's center (ring?) of performance art.

What has enough square footage and ceilings high enough for student circus performers to climb aerial silks, swing from a trapeze, and practice on a tramp wall? A former church.

The teal doors are the only exterior clue that this former church (continuously occupied since 1907) is no longer a house of worship. Courtesy of Joni Hirsch Blackman

Inset: The Aloft website calls the studio "a circus artist's dream come true." Courtesy of Johanna Vargas

NOW IT'S...

Was: First Evangelical Church; First Spanish United Church of Christ

Is: Aloft Circus Arts

Location: 3324 W Wrightwood Ave. (at Kimball)

Tip: Find information on classes, performances, and one-off feature acts for corporate or private events at aloftloft.com.

A Pair of Shoe Factories

The city of big shoulders also had big shoe factories, as many as twenty-nine in 1923 producing nearly nine million pairs of shoes each year. The city was home to twenty-eight tanneries, thanks to the Union Stock Yards, offering plenty of quality leather for shoe making.

One of Chicago's premier shoe manufacturers was founded in 1892 by Milton Florsheim, whose German immigrant father, Sigmund, became a shoemaker after settling in Chicago in 1862. Florsheim & Co. operated out of existing buildings until 1900, when the company built its first factory west of the Chicago River at Adams and Clinton. It no longer exists.

The company grew quickly, partly thanks to its "French" square-toed men's shoes popular with WWI veterans accustomed to wide combat boots as opposed to the pointed-toed men's shoes of the era.

Florsheim built two new factories in rapid succession. A four-story building at 3927 W Belmont Ave. in 1919; the second, six-story building opened in 1926, totaling six-hundred-thousand-square-feet of manufacturing space along Belmont.

By the end of World War II, Florsheim was one of the top ten shoe manufacturers in the country, but shoe manufacturing largely moved overseas by the 1970s.

In 1987, the Belmont Avenue factory was sold to Records Management Services, Inc. but in 2005, shoes returned—this time in closets of new residents of Shoemaker Lofts. The condominiums retained the mostly glass exterior, gutting all but the exposed-brick walls inside.

In 1949, Florsheim had constructed a new downtown facility, diagonally across from its original factory. Its views of Union Station came in handy when the International Style U-shaped building was converted into condominiums in 1997.

"The company at present is making eight thousand pairs of men's shoes daily. With the annex, it will turn out between eleven thousand and twelve thousand pairs," reported the October 28, 1923, *Tribune*.

Designed by Alfred Alschuler, who believed industrial buildings should have natural light, this reinforced concrete and glass structure, built between 1924 and 1926, was known as a "daylight" factory. Courtesy of Shoemaker Lofts

Inset: Shoemaker Loft front door shows original name. Courtesy of Shoemaker Lofts

The Canal Street building was "the first major Chicago structure to emphatically embrace the design elements of European modernism," according to 1983's AIA guide. Many, of course, followed in Florsheim's footsteps.

NOW IT'S...

Was: Florsheim Shoe Factory

Is: Shoemaker Lofts/Metropolitan Place

Location: 3963 W Belmont Ave. /130 S Canal St.

Tip: The Belmont entrance featured a horizontal terra-cotta plaque with green letters spelling out "The Florsheim Shoe Co.," which remains.

Flop-Flip: Hotel to Office

In the early 1900s, residents moved to Chicago in droves; railroads brought a massive influx. Fort Dearborn filled a void—not as fancy as some, but nicer than low-rent flophouses. "Clientele were serious businessmen with specialized needs ... an image that was modern, functional, and tasteful enough to impress potential customers, yet without the "frills" that would make prices prohibitive." Cost? $2.50 a night.

Across from the LaSalle Street Station, two blocks from the old Grand Central Station and steps from the "L," it was the "only hotel in Chicago with direct transportation at its doors to all parts of the city," according to the NRHP form. The $1.2 million building was then located in the wholesale garment and textile district, near the "financial interests of LaSalle Street."

The five hundred hotel rooms, opened in March 1914, were equipped with toilets, and half of them also had baths. Behind the reception desk, the two eight-by-seventeen-foot Fort Dearborn murals were painted by local artist Edgar S. Cameron (also the *Chicago Tribune*'s art critic at the time.)

By 1982, the place had deteriorated. Newspapers reported a twenty-year-old hotel resident was stabbed to death by her roommate, twenty-three, after the younger woman accused the older of borrowing clothes without permission.

The following year an $8 million renovation began, restoring the exterior, gutting the interior and renaming it the Traders Building—referring to its proximity to the Chicago Board Options Exchange (across the street) and the Board of Trade (kitty-corner). Offices were filled mostly by traders and attorneys who moved into the fifteen floors above. The lobby bar features original appointments such as a massive wood fireplace.

The exterior and lobby were converted into a nightclub while shooting a 1991 made-for-TV movie, *Against the Mob*, which, though set in 1930s New York, was the "right vintage."

Designed by Holabird & Roche, the Fort Dearborn Hotel's 500 rooms had toilets and 250 baths. Courtesy of Curt Teich & Co.

Inset: This 1963 postcard noted the hotel's air-conditioned lobby and rooms, excellent restaurant, and cocktail lounge, and promised that the Dearborn was "[w]here you will get the Red Carpet Treatment." Photos Courtesy of Curt Teich & Co.

Capping the central light court (not open to the public) with a skylight created an atrium, inspiration for the name of the building cited as 1985's best historic renovation in Chicago—trading up from middle of the road.

NOW IT'S...

Was: Fort Dearborn Hotel, The Traders Building

Is: LaSalle Atrium Building

Location: 401 S LaSalle St.

Tip: The historic lobby features rich wood everywhere, a player piano, a detailed, coffered ceiling, and two historic Fort Dearborn murals.

Read About Goldblatt's Here

Polish immigrants Simon and Hannah Goldblatt settled near the intersection of Ashland, Division, and Milwaukee Avenues in 1903, when the area was known as "Polish downtown." The following year, the Goldblatts opened a small grocery store, the Polska Skalp, on Chicago Avenue, living above the store with their children.

Eleven years later, the eldest boys—Maurice, twenty-one, and Nathan, nineteen—opened a small dry goods store down the street, with a loan from their parents and money they'd saved as department store clerks. Younger brothers Louis, eleven, and Joel, seven, helped on weekends. Focused on working-class customers' schedules, they were open 7 a.m. to 9 p.m. and offered affordable prices.

The combination worked so well that the store's size doubled onto an adjoining lot within a year—the first of seven expansions there in thirteen years that eventually spanned from Ashland to Paulina Avenues.

The city's landmark application for the Alfred-Alschuler-designed building noted, "From a twenty-five-foot-wide storefront in 1914 to a 275-foot-long block front in 1928—[Goldblatt's] was integral to the very development of this commercial district. The five-story facade dominates the streetscape in virtually every direction."

One of the country's oldest large neighborhood department stores, it was the first in a regional chain of more than three dozen Goldblatt's stores. Known nationwide for retailing innovations—including displaying merchandise out in the open instead of behind counters—they offered more than one hundred departments, such as automotive parts, beauty salons, garden centers, pet stores, and uniforms.

Nathan died in 1944; Maurice retired to raise money for cancer and heart research. The younger brothers expanded to the suburbs and small Midwestern towns. In 1981, Goldblatt's filed for bankruptcy. This, the first store, was the last closed, in 1996.

The two Goldblatt Bros. buildings are among the best-preserved, surviving examples of early neighborhood department stores in Chicago or the U.S.

This 1927 scene symbolized what the East Village Association didn't want to disappear. Their 1996 flyer: "We'd lose a solid building that contributes to the character of our urban neighborhood." Courtesy of Gladys Alcazar-Anselmo

Inset: When Gladys Alcazar-Anselmo heard Goldblatt's would be torn down, she called Landmarks Illinois and asked questions. In the end, LI learned from EVA's passionate determination how well grassroots efforts can work. Courtesy of Gladys Alcazar-Anselmo

The building was slated for demolition, but protesting neighbors saved it. The East Village Association was honored by the state Landmarks Preservation Council for its intense efforts, saying, "These people never gave up." Great lesson for any library book.

NOW IT'S...

Was: Goldblatt Bros. Department Store

Is: West Town City Offices; Chicago Public Library branch

Location: 1613-35 W Chicago Ave.

Tip: The original Goldblatt Bros. logo is atop the three-story building; the library lobby's marble floor came from the store.

Go West, Young Talk Show Host

West Washington Street? Where's that?

Fans of Oprah Winfrey's mega-hit talk show found it, ecstatic to be standing in line to join her studio audience when Harpo Studios opened in 1989. Moving from WLS-TV's Loop studios, Oprah's presence transformed the then-little-known Near West Side neighborhood. Winfrey had arrived in Chicago in 1984, to host WLS-TV's A.M. Chicago show. Within three years, ratings for the retitled *Oprah Winfrey Show*, national as of 1986, surpassed those of Phil Donahue and became the most popular talk show on TV. Harpo (Oprah backwards) was founded that year, eventually producing miniseries and documentaries, as well as the iconic chatfest.

For twenty-five years, Harpo Studios powered neighborhood revitalization while Oprah transformed daytime TV. Winfrey ended the show in 2011; Harpo Studios was briefly home to Rosie O'Donnell's talk show and other TV shows.

Though Harpo is gone, its legacy endures. Back in 1988, officials speculated Winfrey's studio could encourage filmmaking in Chicago.

"Previously, there was no desire to build any sets here," an Illinois Film Office spokesperson told Crain's. "They would shoot the exteriors here, and then immediately head back to LA. The space they needed to do their building simply didn't exist."

Harpo changed all that, and countless television shows and movies film in Chicago regularly. In 2016, the building was demolished to clear space for a new corporate headquarters for another American icon—McDonald's. Moving from its longtime home in suburban Oak Brook,

Purchasing the former building at this site, Oprah became the third woman in American entertainment history to own her own studio and the first black woman to own her own television and film production complex.

Harpo Studios before the final taping of The Oprah Winfrey Show," May 24, 2011. The Golden Arches company has big shoes to fill as a neighbor; Oprah once sent a case of Dom Perignon to next-door residents. Courtesy of AP Photo/Paul Beaty

McDonald's nine-story, six-hundred-thousand-square-foot building opens in 2018.

Oprah's legacy will be incorporated in the new building, developers said. Maybe not the couch Tom Cruise jumped on, but something to evoke memories of Chicago media professionals who launched their careers there, and audience members whose mornings were defined by countless "Aha" moments.

NOW IT'S...

Was: Harpo Studios, Home of the Oprah Winfrey Show

Is: Headquarters, McDonald's Corporation

Location: was 1058 W Washington St. now 110 N Carpenter

Tip: "We're grateful to [Oprah]," Alderman Walter Burnett Jr. said in 2016. The "once gritty" West Loop is now a "safe and cool area, and she was an early pioneer."

Cultural Folks Love Books and Music

Hild Regional Library was the second regional library in the Chicago Public Library system. Retiring at the age of sixty-four left the still-useful art deco building empty for a decade until the Old Town School of Folk Music filled it with melodies.

A $10 million renovation turned the old library into a center for musicians of all ages and levels to learn from staff and each other, creating music and dance of various cultures.

Dedicated on September 18, 1998, with a concert by Joni Mitchell and Peter Yarrow, the school touted its "finest facility in North America for the study and presentation of folk and traditional music forms." The forty-three-thousand-square-foot building features a 435-seat, semi-circular concert hall, a computer music center, recording studio, the "Different Strummer" music store, and a popular cafe/student hangout where there used to be book stacks and quiet reading rooms.

Some library remnants were left intact, including two Works Progress Administration murals from the former children's reading room. One was remounted in Maurer Concert Hall and the other in a second-floor gallery, the library's former print shop. "Frederick H. Hild Regional Branch" remains above the front door, as do five architectural medallions along the Lincoln Avenue facade.

The vintage structure had been considered for use as a warehouse, but the community balked. The first vision as a nonprofit community art space never attracted funding, but Old Town's need to expand struck the right chord.

Opened in 1931, named for Chicago's second librarian, Frederick H. Hild. The library closed in 1985 when Lincoln Square's Conrad Sulzer (a Ravenswood pioneer) library opened down the street.

Frederick Hild was Chicago's chief librarian from 1887 to 1909. Designed by architect Pierre Blouke, the library named for Hild features "a discreet owl (as) the only playful element," says the AIA guide. Courtesy of Chicago Public Library

Inset: After Hild's 1998 renovation, Chicago Tribune Architecture Critic Blair Kamin wrote, "It seems as if the folk center was meant to be in the old library, a minor gem with a simple but powerful Art Deco front." Courtesy of Joni Hirsch Blackman

Post-renovations, *Chicago Tribune* architecture critic Blair Kamin said the "terrific little building" ranked as "one of the finest reuses of an existing interior in Chicago in a long time."

Perfect refrain for a lilting former library.

NOW IT'S...

Was: Frederick Hild Library

Is: Old Town School of Music

Location: 4544 N Lincoln Ave.

Tip: Internationally known touring artists like the late Pete Seeger, as well as local artists, school staff, and students perform most weekends and Wednesday nights.

Money, Drugs, and Booze

For 21st century customers used to banking at an ATM or online, a bank like this one, completed at a cost of $1 million in 1925, is from not just another century, but truly from another era. Home Bank and Trust Company's sign hung at this corner just four short years after its elaborate construction, another bank derailed by the Great Depression.

United American Trust and Savings Bank took over, but it, too failed the following year. The Milwaukee Avenue National Bank opened there in 1934, changing its name in 1946 to Manufacturers National Bank, then Manufacturers Bank in 1984, later shortened to MB Financial.

Like its banks, the Karl Vitzthum-designed building has had its ups and downs. Downs include the year many windows were bricked in—1968, the year Chicago hosted a volatile Democratic convention (bricks were a way to protect the windows). Those were taken out shortly after the building was sold in 2004. But it wasn't until 2011 that CVS Pharmacy completely restored this striking structure embellished with its intricately carved low-relief sculpture all around.

The stained-glass ceiling and massive columns connected with arches at the second-floor level make it easy to imagine this space as the dramatic former banking hall it was—even with the more mundane pharmacy inventory throughout. Even more impressive is the bank's former basement bar/restaurant with its gleaming vault and safe deposit boxes. Truly, there's no place like the former "Home."

Until recently, The Bedford Restaurant and Bar, named after the Indiana town where the building's limestone was quarried, occupied the basement and featured former private banking booths repurposed as ladies' bathroom stalls.

Wiebolt Construction company took this photo just after the bank was built in 1926. Courtesy of Chicago History Museum

Inset: The winged angels in bas relief over the front door of the CVS pharmacy could refer to the people who renovated this former bank to make a real investment in the community. Courtesy of Joni Hirsch Blackman

NOW IT'S...

Was: Home Bank and Trust Company Building

Is: CVS Pharmacy

Location: 1200-08 N Ashland Ave. / 1600-12 W Division St.

Tip: The gold-veined marble along the staircase came from the bank's old teller counters.

On Top of A Railroad, All Covered in Green

For more than one hundred years, it was the eyesore along Lake Michigan: acres cluttered with Illinois Central Railroad tracks and parking lots, as ugly as it is now breathtaking. Mayor Richard M. Daley, stuck in the dentist's chair overlooking the scene in 1997, wondered, "What are we going to do with that?"

Millennium Park was the answer. Talk about "no little plans." Even Chicago's most famous visionary, Daniel Burnham himself, knowing the city didn't control the railroad section, didn't press to transform that northwest corner in 1909—he simply designed Grant Park around it.

Developing empty lakefront land had been technically prohibited since 1837, but one section was given by the city to the Illinois Central Railroad in 1852. The right-of-way was payback after ICR constructed a breakwater in the lake to protect the swath of open space east of Michigan Avenue called "Lake Park" (and Boul Mich itself) from washing away during winter storms.

That right-of-way spread like a virus. Train-centered construction—terminals, freight facilities, switchyards—sprang up and crowded the space between Michigan Avenue and the lake.

In 1871, the future Millennium Park briefly became a ballpark. The National League Chicago White Stockings (early Chicago Cubs) played in the Union baseball grounds between Michigan Avenue and Illinois Central tracks, north of Madison Street. Home plate was along Randolph Street.

Daley's park became a possible dream thanks to the city's 1996 lawsuit noting the land was no longer being used primarily for railroad purposes so should be returned to the city.

Built on top of a parking garage, a Metra station, and still-operating railroad tracks, the park sparked billions of dollars in construction and renovation of residential, office, and hotels nearby.

In 1943 (and before, and after) a person standing on the famed Michigan Avenue street wall could barely see Lake Michigan past the mess of train tracks and railroad cars in front of the buildings. Courtesy of Library of Congress

NOW IT'S...

Was: Illinois Central Railroad tracks/Union baseball field

Is: Millennium Park

Location: Between Michigan Avenue and Columbus Drive, from Randolph Street to Monroe Street

Tip: Millennium Park won the 2009 Rudy Bruner Award for Urban Excellence, and regularly rank as one of the top tourist spots among American parks.

Critics called the six-year project a nightmare, opening four years late and at three times the original $140 million budget. But since opening on July 16, 2004, the seventeen-acre park, aka the world's largest rooftop garden, is considered priceless (by locals and tourists alike).

Hello Down There!

Years before penalty-riddled cell phone contracts, Chicago was misled by a contract for land line phones with Illinois Telephone and Telegraph Company. Authorized by city hall in 1898 to build and operate one of the country's first automatic dial-type telephone systems, IT&T's stated plan was to dig tunnels just big enough for installation of underground cables.

Work was stopped four years later when city officials realized these passageways were big enough to walk through—seven feet tall, horseshoe-shaped concrete tunnels. The company convinced officials the city would benefit from a transportation system mirroring city streets below ground with tracks for small mine-trolley-like freight cars. The unique sixty-mile electric railroad system brought coal and freight to Loop buildings and was used to haul out ashes from coal-burning equipment and to move mail.

Oh, and, a 1910 article noted: "The bores also contain the cables of one of the telephone companies." So much for original intention. By that time, IT&T's name even morphed into Illinois Tunnel Company, then Chicago Tunnel Company.

The $40 million project lost money from nearly the beginning, worsening when truck competition increased. The Chicago Tunnel went bankrupt in 1959.

Used sporadically afterwards, the tunnels were mostly forgotten until 1992's infamous Loop flood was caused by contractors installing pilings in the Chicago River. They didn't realize it at the time, but their equipment hit the top of the tunnel, and river water began to leak in. On April 13, the leak became a flood (in the end, some 120 million gallons.) When first water, then fish turned up in the Merchandise Mart's basement, the river was the obvious source.

George Jackson spent so many hours overseeing the 24/7 tunnel construction, his family moved above the tunnels in 1904, turning the fifth floor of IT&T's Monroe Street building into their home.

Sixty miles of freight tunnels run forty feet under Chicago's streets—no other American city has a similar system. Courtesy of V.O. Hammon Publishing Co.

Inset: Typical intersection in 1904. Courtesy of Bruce Moffatt Collection

A radio reporter noticed rotating river waters resembling "a giant drain" near the Kinzie Street bridge, sparking a rush to plug the hole, to turn off electricity to Loop buildings, and evacuate workers. Well, IT&T *did* promise to clear traffic off city streets.

NOW IT'S...

Was: Illinois Telephone & Telegraph Co. Tunnels

Is: Now used for power and communications cables

Location: Forty feet below almost every street in the Loop—from Halsted Street to Michigan Avenue, from Illinois Street to 15th Street.

Tip: The 1992 flood alerted people to the tunnels' existence. Tunnel entrances were sealed with steel, waterproof doors.

For Women, Athletic and Catholic

Standing next to a "sugar and paste" miniature of the proposed clubhouse in 1923, officers of the Illinois Women's Athletic Club likely never imagined their sweet seventeen-story tower would someday house Hershey's Chocolate World. (OK, they probably never imagined anything like Hershey's Chocolate World, regardless.) But theirs is a story of grand plans quickly dissolved.

The Gothic skyscraper was "a long-cherished dream," the 1926 *Tribune* noted of the eight-year-old club housed in an old residence. It was razed to make space for the "only club of its kind in the city, the largest woman's athletic club in the world."

The keynote for October 20, 1926's opening day was "What Diana desires—she usually gets." The "ultra-modern, thoroughly feminine, and completely beautiful."

Resident rooms towered over a "large swimming tank" and a gymnasium was constructed with "extensive equipment, where also are to be held the reducing classes which bid fair to be a most popular innovation in club circles." Also included: bowling alleys, billiards rooms, Turkish baths, steam rooms, dining room, and a ballroom—for 3,500 women members.

By June 1933, the club's building was in receivership. In 1935, six floors were rented by the Illinois Club for Catholic Women, headed by Mrs. Frank J. Lewis. Remodeling added a two-hundred-seat chapel on the 15th floor, a cocktail bar and lounge, and fifth-floor dormitories "for business women of moderate income." Four floors housed a women's hotel.

A 1926 *Tribune* article gushed: "Every possible accessory for enhancing feminine pulchritude has been anticipated in the beauty parlor—with its furnishings in black patent leather and chintz, against creamy yellow walls."

The Illinois Women's Athletic Lounge is pictured here. The dining hall was called "The Chicago Room," featuring Currier and Ives reproductions of Chicago scenes in twelve murals depicting early Chicago history. Courtesy of chicagopc.info

Inset: As the Illinois Women's Athletic Club, members had a standing rule that men were only allowed in the building at the invitation of club members, but were not welcome on the three residential floors. Courtesy of Loyola University Chicago

The U.S. Navy took over the building when World War II began. Midshipmen attending training school and sailors on housing allowances moved into the shore patrol barracks; a naval jail was constructed on the third floor.

After the war, those window bars were removed when philanthropist Frank J. Lewis purchased the building, donating it to Loyola and the ICCW.

The old brig morphed into the commerce library, thus giving future students a nearly legitimate reason to complain they were locked up studying.

NOW IT'S...

Was: Illinois Women's Athletic Club

Is: Loyola University Lewis Towers (Hershey's Chocolate World has moved out)

Location: 820 N Michigan Ave.

Tip: Above the building doorway is a relief of Diana, the Roman goddess of the hunt, and her dog.

Stellar Cellar

Ralph Jansen had always loved Sir Walter Scott's *Ivanhoe*, a magical castle tale set in medieval England. 'Tis said the former waiter opened his Ivanhoe speakeasy—which grew to include a series of dining rooms and bars set around a garden—with his brother, Harold.

Newspaper columnists of the day called it the place for "visiting conventioneers." Most popular was the medieval-themed cellar, accessed by a "shaky elevator" that made the trip down seem much farther than it actually was. Patrons exited the elevator, weaving through a labyrinthian tunnel lined with skeletons, then were enveloped with an atmosphere of rousing good fun: "Boozy evenings of sing-a-longs, dancing, and magic."

Jansen died in 1956. His nephew, Richard, continued despite a dynamite bomb in 1964 that damaged the entrance. In 1966, a six-hundred-seat theater-in-the-round matching the medieval English style was added, connecting to the restaurant. Considered one of the city's hottest theaters through the early 1970s, it featured well-known actors of the time, including Zsa Zsa Gabor, Rita Moreno, Jessica Tandy, Joan Fontaine, Piper Laurie, and Christopher Walken.

In 1975, business sagged and it was regretfully reported that "after fifty-four years of attracting tourists, conventioneers, prom kids, movie stars, and visiting dignitaries, the Ivanhoe Restaurant has closed." Dramatic detail: the theater was featuring *The Last Straw*.

Harold Binstein acquired the former restaurant in 1978, and reopened it as Gold Standard Liquors, later renamed Binny's Beverage Depot, in 1999.

The theater reopened briefly as The Wellington, but a fire in 1977 lowered the curtain again. In 1982, Douglas Bragan added a theater in the former courtyard and another small one in the old Catacombs. Successful for years, many noted "it will be missed" when it closed in 2000.

"We've taken our friends on a catacomb tour ... the scene always reminds us of a fraternity open house at homecoming," quipped a 1955 *Tribune* columnist.

Owner Ralph Jansen' who died in 1956, had been a waiter at a beer hall and restaurant until Prohibition, when he opened the Ivanhoe as a speakeasy. Inset: The dungeon-like catacombs that was actually at normal basement's distance below street level was dismantled in 1974 in hopes of installing a never-realized disco.

NOW IT'S...

Was: The Ivanhoe restaurant/theater

Is: Binny's Liquors

Location: 3000 N Clark St.

Tip: The old exposed-brick catacombs, featuring a wine cellar and Prohibition memorabilia, have been restored for tastings and other events.

Michael Binstein bought the former theater and gutted it, turning the entire space into a fifty-thousand-square-foot fine wine and specialty foods superstore, sometimes advertised as Binny's Ivanhoe Castle. These days it's the boozing, not the show, that must go on.

You Need a Loft

Baking was the main objective at 1001-1025 West Randolph Street back in 1884, where the Kennedy Baking Co., later owned by American Biscuit, rebuilt their factory after a fire. Folded into the National Biscuit Co. in 1898, the company—busy producing cookies and crackers—needed another ten-oven bakery, which was constructed across the way, at 1000 W Washington in 1902, to produce its Uneeda line of biscuits and, for those who gave a fig, fig bars.

The new factory was state-of-the-art, with two-story brick baking ovens. The building featured a six-story tower with (now removed) pergola; in 1915, an addition was constructed to the east end, enlarging the bakery to the full block on Washington. Approximately 1,300 employees worked at the two-building complex for years, but after World War II, the company moved to newer bakeries on the city's south side.

The catchier-named Nabisco sold the buildings in 1954 to textbook wholesaler J.W. Wilcox & Follett Co.—finally, some good reading material to go with the snacks. The warehouses held as many as 20 million textbooks with 96,000 different titles. The renamed Follett Corp. repaired books in its West Washington Street headquarters to return them as used books for sale in its college and university bookstores.

But Follett, too, found its future someplace else—in this case, the suburbs. The company sold the buildings in the mid-1990s and the combined 497,000 square feet were converted into 180 residential units. Residents moved in 1996 and 1997.

Uneeda Biscuit's slogan was: "Lest you forget, we say it yet, Uneeda Biscuit!" Of course, in modern times that morphed into "You need a Car!" Right, Oprah?

Located next door to the old Harpo Studios, Oprah Winfrey filmed three "Meet My Neighbors" segments here; one involved designer Nate Berkus styling twelve balconies.

Before this building was constructed in 1884 as Kennedy Baking Co., the land was owned by druggist Deacon Philo Carpenter ... (an aha moment: Carpenter Streetl) Designed by architects Treat & Folz, waxed paper liners were invented here, keeping future crackers dry in countless packages. Courtesy of chicagopc.info

Inset: Several parts of Nabisco's original ovens hang in the lobby of the residence where then-senator Obama once held a fundraiser. Courtesy of Joni Hirsch Blackman

NOW IT'S ...

Was: Kennedy Baking Co., American Biscuit Co., National Biscuit Co. (Nabisco)

Is: 1000 W Washington Lofts

Location: 1000 W Washington but best entrance is 115 N Carpenter

Tip: Celebrity-spotting was a daily event in the *Oprah* days; now cast members of TV shows *Chicago PD* and *Chicago Med* live here.

Rooftops and Bridges

Fitting, perhaps, that a building constructed on the site of a bloody massacre (1812) would have some troubles. First, the structure's design had to take into account a small piece of the land whose owner wouldn't sell. Designing literally around the 24 × 50-foot structure on Michigan Avenue, Alfred Alschuler managed to do so by creating a light court above it—and still win the city's "best new building" Gold Medal in the north central district for 1923. At the last minute, the small building was acquired, but Alschuler didn't change his plans, he just replaced the demolished building with a five-story wing and left the light court above it. No matter: the irregularly-shaped land already had required an unusual, trapezoidal shaped building.

Then the namesake company of the twenty-one-story Beaux Arts building decided just before it was completed that it wouldn't move its headquarters to the $4 million building's sixteenth to twentieth floors after all, instead choosing to go to New York. Local London Guarantee workers did move in as did General Motors. Leo Burnett was a tenant until 1957.

But the land will always be most famous for its first structures: the log buildings of Fort Dearborn, established by President Thomas Jefferson and named for Secretary of War Henry Dearborn. After the 1812 destruction, the fort was rebuilt in 1816, then torn down in 1858; the northeast corner of London Guarantee features a small plaque in commemoration. The British insurance company's Corinthian-columned structure with its original name carved above the door also sports a unique domed cupola at the top.

From 1946 to 1976, the ground floor was home to the first London House, a celebrated jazz club. In 1960 it was known as the Stone Container Building, with offices there through 1986. Crain Communications

In December 1922, descendants of Chicago settlers watched as the great-grandson of the Captain who commanded 1803's Fort Dearborn laid the London Guarantee & Accident Building's cornerstone.

One of four historic structures bordering the DuSable Bridge, the belvedere at the top is a counterpoint to the Wrigley Building's tower across the river. Courtesy of Art Institute

Inset: London House was the name of the ground-floor jazz club nearly as famous as the big names who played there from 1946 to 1976. Courtesy of Joni Hirsch Blackman

populated the building from 1986 until 2013, when it was sold to new owners thinking "hotel."

Opened in 2016, LondonHouse's rooftop bar immediately became a must-see vantage point, and the lobby Bridges bar has an unusual view of the Chicago River bridges that is simply the bee's knees.

NOW IT'S...

Was: London Guarantee & Accident

Is: LondonHouse Chicago hotel

Location: 360 N Michigan Ave./enter at 85 E Wacker Dr.

Tip: LondonHouse's popular tri-level rooftop bar takes reservations; the belvedere can be rented by the hour for special events, including proposals.

A Theatre by Any Bank Name Is Just as Majestic

In 1906, the twenty-story Majestic Office Building & Theater opened as a Vaudeville house with 2,500 seats, featuring such circuit luminaries as Eddie Foy and Harry Houdini. The city's first million-dollar-plus venue, it closed in the early 1930s, a victim of the Depression, and sat dark for about a dozen years.

New York's Shubert group bought the building in 1945, naming it after a brother, Sam, who had died in a train wreck. A remodel retained much of the original design, and the Sam S. Shubert Theatre reopened to host the major plays of the times—*Carousel, South Pacific, Guys and Dolls, Hair, A Chorus Line*. Pre-Broadway world premieres staged there include *Movin' Out, Spamalot*—the last show to play there before the Shubert name disappeared—and *Kinky Boots*.

In 2004, the Nederlander organization (which had purchased the theater in 1991) announced a major multi-million-dollar renovation of the historic theater, together with a re-naming purchased by financial partner LaSalle Bank. Two thousand brand-new seats, a lobby expansion, and a full restoration took place in 2005. Perhaps most noticeable to patrons, the restroom size was tripled and, most appreciated by the actors, new drywall and plumbing were installed backstage. Historic elements hidden for fifty years were uncovered and restored in various areas, helping the theater live up to its original name.

The LaSalle Bank Theatre reopened with eighty fewer seats in 2006, only to be re-named the Bank of America Theatre two years later when the bank was acquired. In February 2016, the marquee was changed to PrivateBank Theatre. Names can change, but bank on this: the theater is still majestic.

Surprise ending! Removal of a dropped ceiling in the outer lobby during the 2005 renovation revealed a previously unknown two-story space ringed with classical colonnades.

The Majestic Theatre opened as a venue for primarily vaudeville entertainment, seating almost 2,500 but occasionally screening movies as well. Courtesy of V. O. Hammon Publishing Co.

Inset: The Shubert Theater from 1945 to 2004. The 1906 office building/theater was designed by architect Edward Krause of Rapp & Rapp. (circa 1966) Courtesy of Chuckman Collection

NOW IT'S...

Was: Majestic Office Building & Theater, Shubert Theater, LaSalle Bank Theater, Bank of America Theater

Is: PrivateBank Theater

Location: 18 W Monroe St.

Tip: In 2005, the upper seventeen floors were converted into a 135-room Hampton Inn that connects to the theater.

Don't Call It Macy's . . . or even Field's

Two green clocks over State Street have been an enduring symbol of Marshall Field & Company, Chicago's iconic department store. The old slogan, "There's Nothing Like It Back Home" signaled its singular reputation: the best in the industry. Generations of grandmothers brought their granddaughters here.

Marshall Field, a Massachusetts farm boy who at twenty-one started as a dry goods clerk in Chicago, was a customer service innovator. He coined "Give the Lady What She Wants" and "The Customer is Always Right." His stores were the first to have a bridal registry, free delivery, and animated window displays. Amenities included food service—the first restaurant began in 1890 when a millinery department employee brought homemade chicken pot pies, keeping customers in the store longer.

What a store it was.

Known as the "Grande Dame" and one of the finest historic department stores in the country, the one-block square property was designed by Daniel H. Burnham. Field acquired all of the properties between State, Washington, and Randolph Streets and Wabash Avenue by 1892 and began construction of the elaborate store to impress visitors to the following year's World's Columbian Exposition.

The rest of the gargantuan structure—at 1.3 million square feet, the largest department store in the world —was completed by 1914. Chicagoans have long loved the ornate Walnut Room restaurant and the Tiffany-designed dome. Outside, the store's first clock was installed on the southwest corner in 1897 to encourage promptness after Field noticed the corner had become a popular meeting spot. The clocks are among the most famous in the country.

The spectacular Tiffany Dome, atop the five-story State and Washington atrium, took fifty men nearly two years to complete. Look up or you'll miss it.

Seen here in 1907, Marshall Field & Co. ranked as one of the 20 largest retail enterprises in the United States at the end of World War II. Courtesy of Library of Congress

Inset: Marshall Field & Company officially never used the word "department," referring to the store's "sections" instead. The confectionary section featured Frango Mints. Courtesy of V. O. Hammon Publishing

After it was converted to Macy's in 2006, some Chicagoans refused to enter the formerly famously forest-green-branded hometown landmark. Life without Marshall Field & Company trucks driving along Chicago's streets has never been quite the same.

NOW IT'S ...

Was: Marshall Field & Co.

Is: Macy's on State

Location: 111 N State St.

Tip: Harry Selfridge, who had worked for Marshall Field, based his English department store, Selfridge's, on what he had learned in Chicago.

Olympic Triangle

Looking like a slice of pie, but with a "wedding cake" exterior, this former bank building was constructed by a 1912 Olympian, the thirty-year president of the International Olympic Committee—Avery Brundage.

Built as the Marshfield Trust and Savings Bank in 1924, that purpose was short-lived.

Despite the Classical Revival style of architecture often chosen to portray a sense of security and permanence for banks, Marshfield, like many banks, didn't survive the Depression. Also known as the National Bond and Mortgage Trust building, it was home to various security ventures, including Lin-Mar Safety Deposit Co. in the 1970s and the Chicago Security Complex.

The basement features the original vault advertised on an early National Bond brochure as "The Safest, Finest, Largest, Most Convenient" bank vault ever offered to north side residents. Though the second four stories were never built, the upper floors—originally doctors' and dentists' offices—have been home to ten condos since a residential conversion in the late 1980s, and can still be accessed by the original marble staircase.

The Lincoln Avenue side features "Brundage Building" above the 3325 entry to the condos. On the Marshfield side, "McKinley Building" was once painted on a window, referencing the Early Edition TV series, one of several movies and tv shows the building has starred in including *Straight Talk*, with Dolly Parton, and as the kidnappers' lair on *Baby's Day Out*, where Hollywood made the building look seven stories high.

Though the architect was William Gibbons Uffendell, it's safe to say the building is more associated with contractor Brundage. The University of Illinois engineering graduate was a discus, pentathlon, and decathlon champion who became president of the U.S. Olympic Association in 1929, then joined the IOC, becoming president in 1952.

A 1923 construction announcement promised "one of the most attractive business structures on Lincoln Avenue," adding that "only four of the proposed eight stories will be built at first."

1980s Building owner George Stylinski offered the building's upper floors as dental and medical suites. Courtesy of Sandy Stylinski

Inset: The Brundage building's ground floor is home to a Arthur Murray Dance Studio at the corner main entrance, beneath a curved, bracketed cornice. A second, straight cornice on Lincoln sits above the words "Brundage Building," the entrance to the residences above. Courtesy of Sandy Stylinski

NOW IT'S...

Was: National Bond and Mortgage Trust, Marshfield Trust and Savings Bank, Chicago Security Complex

Is: The Brundage Building Lofts and Arthur Murray Dance Studio

Location: 3311/3325 N Lincoln Ave.

Tip: The basement bank vault/safe deposit boxes are the centerpiece of an event venue conceived by first floor occupant Arthur Murray.

Dirigible Docking Dome?

The Medinah Athletic Club's distinctive gold-domed flashiness was heralded loudly, but its heyday was brief—bankrupt after the Great Depression, the $8 million luxury men's club closed in 1934.

The *Chicago Tribune* called the landmark's interior "an architectural attempt to trace no less than the course of civilization through a stupendous mix of Greek, Roman, Assyrian, Celtic, medieval, Spanish, and Renaissance styles."

Many floors offered "luxurious living quarters, but fourteen were devoted to athletic pursuits of the 3,500 elite members, the crowning glory being an Olympic-sized swimming pool on the fourteenth floor, one of the highest in the world."

Other highlights included the indoor rifle range, a bowling alley, a twenty-third floor miniature golf course with water hazards, a billiards hall, running track, gymnasium, archery range, and boxing arena. Only the pool remains.

Criticized for "wasteful extravagance" after its April 1929 opening (just six months before the stock market crash), the forty-five-story building featured elaborate artwork, private dining rooms separated by leather-covered, soundproof folding doors, and a two-story elliptically shaped ballroom with North America's then-largest Baccarat crystal chandelier, weighing twelve thousand pounds . . . perhaps the critics had a point.

When the Shriners forfeited ownership in bankruptcy, the building was converted to residential apartments (some athletic facilities still were used). A decade later, actress/swimmer Esther Williams swam in the still-famous pool, complete with rows of seating on the west end.

Bought in 1947 by Sheraton, a second hotel tower to the north was later added. From 1978 it was a Radisson hotel; in 1983, the Continental. Three years later it was closed. InterContinental Hotels and Resorts bought

Rumors that the forty-foot-wide gilded concrete dome was built to moor dirigibles, a plan derailed by the Hindenburg tragedy, are but a logistical blip—the Hindenburg exploded eight years after the building's completion.

Courtesy of InterContinental Hotel Chicago

Inset: The fabulous restoration of the famous Medinah pool. Restoring other rooms included replicating exact details in drapes, carpets, and murals with the help of a former Medinah Club member's yearbook. Courtesy of InterContinental Hotel Chicago

it in 1988 and began what officials said would be "much further than restoration. . . . We want to preserve as much of that architectural beauty as possible . . . museum-quality work."

There's even an actual mini-museum off the lobby. True that.

NOW IT'S...

Was: Medinah Athletic Club, Chicago Towers, Continental Hotel and Town Club, Sheraton, Radisson

Is: Hotel Inter-Continental Chicago

Location: 505 N Michigan Ave.

Tip: The Shriners' greeting is etched inside the south entrance; tiles inlaid in the upper lobby steps to a fountain showcase founders' family crests.

Wedding Registries Can Be Such a Circus

Beware of ghosts of men wearing red fezzes. Chicago's Shriners needed a meeting place/convention center in the early 1900s. But why Islamic mosque-like? The fraternal/social group's official name tells the tale: The Ancient Arabic Order of Nobles of the Mystic Shrine.

Considered one of the grandest Shrine temples in the country, Medinah Temple opened in 1913 on the eastern half of a city block bounded by Wabash, Ontario, State, and Ohio Streets. The exotic onion domes and detailed structure was then, and remains, one of the country's finest examples of Middle Eastern-style architecture.

The interior featured a banquet hall with space for 2,300 to sit and a 4,200-seat auditorium featured legendary acoustics and a ninety-two-rank pipe organ. The yearly Medina Shrine Circus (benefitting the Shriners' philanthropies) was based there, as was the more locally appreciated 25th anniversary of Bozo's Circus in 1986.

Shriners blended a serious philanthropic mission supporting hospitals for children with lighthearted rituals and entertainment. In those days, the Middle East was seen by Westerners as a mystical, indulgent place, so Islamic styles and symbols were all the rage. Networking groups and exotic parties were only open to members, but events from circuses to concerts were open to the public.

Since 2003, it's been filled with bedding, crystal, and china but visitors can still note hints of the Shriner era: stained-glass windows, the domed ceiling, and the outline of a stage. Soon after the Shriners moved to the suburbs, their temple was slated for demolition in favor of a luxury hotel and a forty-story condominium tower.

Twelve hundred impassioned letters to the Landmarks Commission in 1999 saved the "delightfully exotic" structure. Mayor Richard M. Daley

Because of the building's fabulous acoustics, the Chicago Symphony Orchestra recorded more than one hundred performances at the temple.

Architects Huehl & Schmid's original terra cotta onion domes were removed by 1940 because of leaks. Copper-clad domes were replaced in 1954, but were removed again by the mid-1990s. The word "Medinah" in brick appears atop the arched grand entrance on Wabash, which was lined with trees circa 1912. Note the homes farther north. Courtesy of Friedman Properties

Inset: The resplendent result of restoration shows the old Medinah Temple as impressive as before. The neighborhood has certainly changed but one thing remains—Tree Studios can still be seen to the far left, just west of Bloomingdale's. The Shriners had purchased the land from Judge Lambert Tree's estate. Courtesy of Friedman Properties

and a renovation-savvy developer secured $14 million in state and federal grants. The once-deteriorating landmark was gloriously reborn as a bright and unique retail store. (Fez toss.)

NOW IT'S...

Was: Medinah Temple, meeting place, and convention center for Shriners

Is: Bloomingdale's Home Store

Location: 600 N Wabash Ave.

Tip: Enter through the original grand entrance on Wabash midway between Ohio and Ontario; look up at the dome when waiting for the elevators.

Fly 'n' Park

Odd name. It's the most *northerly* of five islands proposed by architect Daniel Burnham in his 1909 Plan of Chicago. Noting "the lakefront, by right, belongs to the people," he envisioned a string of manmade islands, beaches, and playing fields parallel to the south lakefront, between Grant and Jackson Parks. Though none of the other four were built, and this "island" is linked to the mainland, the name remains.

Completed in February 1920, Northerly offers breathtaking views of the lake and skyline. Site of the 1933 World's Fair, officials later briefly considered a "permanent fair"—a casino and amusement park.

The Depression and World War II derailed those plans, leaving a public space until the mid-1940s. A proposal to put the newly formed United Nations' headquarters there went nowhere.

But Merrill C. Meigs, publisher of the *Chicago Herald and Examiner* and former World War I Federal Aircraft Department chair, led the effort to establish a tiny private airport on the island, opening in 1947. An air control tower was added in 1952 and Meigs Field flourished for more than 30 years.

Mayor Richard M. Daley, elected in 1989, always wanted Northerly Island to revert to its original purpose. With Park District support, detailed plans were unveiled in anticipation of the expiration of the city's original fifty-year lease in 1996. Governor Jim Edgar balked and a compromise kept the airport open until 2002 (extended to 2006.)

Then, like a movie scene, at midnight on March 31, 2003, Daley—citing post-9/11 concerns about terrorists using the field to attack downtown—sent bulldozers to the island to tear up the runways. The controversial move was cheered by environmentalists.

"You couldn't do the job we did without what he did," said Mayor Rahm Emmanuel at the park's dedication twelve years later.

"We will look back and say, 'This is incredible.' They won't believe it was all asphalt and concrete out there."—Bob O'Neill, president of the Grant Park Advisory Council, 2003.

Construction crews descended on Meigs Field overnight and dug up large chunks of the lakefront runway on March 31, 2003. Federal authorities, at Mayor Daley's request, had days earlier imposed a no-fly zone over Chicago's business district. Daley had long wanted the airport to revert to a park. Courtesy of AP photo/Brian Kersey

All visitors, not just private-plane travelers, can now experience the ninety-acre lakefront nature park/wildlife sanctuary as it was before Chicago was a city—though a major city is just blocks away.

The former air terminal building is now a visitors' center with a lawn of native flowers and wild prairie grass. And, perhaps, the spirit of Daniel Burnham.

NOW IT'S...

Was: Meigs Field

Is: Northerly Island Park

Location: 1521 S Linn White Dr. (south of Adler Planetarium, east of Soldier Field)

Tip: Music in the Park: Huntington Bank Pavilion's stage on the north end offers summer concerts with seating and lawn space.

Mail Order by the River

When Montgomery Ward and Company moved from Michigan Avenue to the east bank of the Chicago River's north branch, newspapers called the surprising relocation "one of the most important and significant real estate developments of recent years ... the event is thought to promise a most important future for this section."

Ward's massive eight-story national headquarters, with an elbow-like bend conforming to the river shoreline, was reported "to be the biggest structure under [one] roof in the world."

The country's oldest mail order company—a concept invented by Montgomery Ward—added an administration building next door, to the south, in 1929. The structure was lauded for its concealed fire escapes and heating system that "will not send forth great clouds of smoke into Chicago's skies." A twelve-story tower was topped with a statue that remains, called *The Spirit of Progress*. A retail store occupied the entire ground floor while upstairs, offices relocated from the original building. The sprawling mail order building, added on to three times, was then used as a warehouse.

In 1974—the same year rival mail-order giant Sears moved across Chicago into its new 110-story tower—Ward's national headquarters moved approximately sixty feet east, into a twenty-six-story modern building with a community center. The company's purchasing department moved into the former Administration Building.

Bankrupt in 1998, the two newer Montgomery Ward buildings were converted into residences. The old mail order house became a mixed-use development—much of which is Groupon's headquarters, but all of which remains what it was at the start: a powerful and significant presence on the Chicago River.

This mail order building wasn't just big, but beautiful: "One of the most powerful works of utilitarian architecture that our building art has produced," said architectural historian Carl Condit.

Montgomery Ward's mail-order building contained miles of chutes and conveyors and storage lofts, allowing workers to fill the thousands of orders received daily. The exterior's distinctive horizontal red brick had been painted white sometime before this 1949 photo. Courtesy of Chicago History Museum, Hedrich-Blessing Collection

Inset: Historians say the secret to Ward's success was simple and set a standard for the later mail order industry: "Be honest, give good value, and always let the customer be the judge." Courtesy of Joni Hirsch Blackman

NOW IT'S...

Was: Montgomery Ward & Co. Mail Order House, Administration Building, and new Headquarters

Is: 600 West (office); One River Place (residential); The Montgomery (residential)

Location: 600 W Chicago Ave.; 758 N Larabee St.; 535 W Chicago Ave.

Tip: "Watchdog of the Lakeshore," Aaron Montgomery Ward financed court battles to keep Lake Michigan's shoreline building free and accessible to the people.

Sports Department: Every Floor!

Sports equipment was in Morrie Mages's blood. He worked alongside his father and three brothers in their Maxwell Street sporting goods store. A law degree from U of I was within reach in 1938—he quit with just a year to go—but he returned to the family business instead.

By the early 1950s, five Mages Sporting Goods stores operated throughout the city and suburbs. Youngest brother Morrie became the face of *Mages Playhouse*, a late-night movie show on WGN-TV, appearing in commercials with then-Cubs broadcaster Jack Brickhouse.

"Internal conflicts" ensued and Mages Sporting Goods Co.—then fourteen stores and other offshoots—was sold in 1960.

Post-sale investments left Mages needing a job. In 1968, he opened a small sporting goods shop on Chicago Avenue. The same model—low-cost, irregular and "going out of business" merchandise, regular purchases from manufacturers, and "pro-only" items—worked again.

By November 1971, his *Chicago Tribune* ad announced the new store at 620 North Lasalle Street, which opened with two floors and a lower level. Mages first rented the building, then bought it, renovating it floor by floor.

Larry Mages, Morrie's son, remembers Arthur Wirtz's Blackhawks hockey team office in the building at the time.

Resembling a sports column, the regular *Tribune* ad had a small photo of Mages and the headline "Sport Shots by Morrie Mages." One column notes: "*I've never seen so many skis, boots, jackets, tennis rackets and golf equipment (sic) in my life. That could be a quote from every person who ever walks into Morrie Mages Sports at 609 N Lasalle Street.*"

Known for his "Mad Marathon" eighteen-hour sales three times each year at his "World's No. 1 Sports Department Store" and "World's Largest

Built in 1906 for Chicago Flexible Shaft Co., the building was sold in 1916 to W.F. McLaughlin Coffee. Maj. Frederic McLaughlin, owner of the Blackhawks at the time, had the team's office there.

Customers lined up for one of the eighteen-hour sales in, as the side of the building proclaims: "The number one sports department store in the world!" Courtesy of Lili Ann Mages Zisook

Sporting Goods Store," the colorful Mages loved to get on the microphone in the eight-story, eighty-thousand-square-foot store and heckle customers into buying more during the 18 hours (6 a.m.- midnight) of the sale. He wanted his store to be a fun place to shop. "People want to buy in a lively atmosphere," he often said. In 1987, the seventy-one-year-old Mages put down his microphone, selling to MC Sporting Goods. He died a year later. Brickhouse said of his "close and dear friend" in the eulogy: "He had a great personality, and he just loved to use that public address system."

It was six years before the Mages name was taken off the iconic floor-numbered building at Lasalle and Ontario, first replaced by Sportmart in 1994 and then by Sports Authority.

Empty in 2016, owners expect the property to be renovated, although it is zoned for up to seventeen stories. A faint echo of Morrie's enthusiastic voice may reverberate throughout, either way.

NOW IT'S . . .

Was: Chicago Flexible Shaft; WF McLaughlin & Co. "Manor House" Coffee; Morrie Mages Sporting Goods; Sportmart; Sports Authority

Is: Empty

Location: 620 N Lasalle St.

Tip: Athletes and broadcasters cast their handprints in concrete along the Ontario Street exterior wall comprising Mages' hall of fame, which remains.

Motel Tell All

Downtown Chicago's hotel boom seems to have no end, but on the outskirts of the north side of town, a somewhat different type of accommodation is hanging on.

Motel Row began in the 1950s thanks to two things: a well-traveled local stretch of U.S. 41 and Chicago's prohibition against motels being reversed in 1953 (no free ride: a motel tax was introduced at the same time). The highway that still runs from Michigan's upper peninsula all the way to Miami was once a popular path to travel through the country. Five miles of that highway is Lincoln Avenue. As many as fourteen motels were built there between 1955 and 1967, before Interstate highways diverted much of the traveling public (aka the plot of the kids' movie *Cars*).

The once-busy motels deteriorated and then began attracting a crowd that typically is attracted to dilapidated motels. Some, like traveling bands, were just looking for a cheap place to flop for the night; some used the rooms like apartments and stayed for months or years. Illegal activity wasn't unusual and negative newspaper headlines followed, as did community calls for something to be done.

A two-for-one solution combined Mayor Richard M. Daley's late 1990s plan to open new police stations and libraries with a move to condemn properties no one would fight to keep around, such as seedy motels with poor reputations. The Spa, the Riverside, and the Acres were demolished by 2000, replaced by a police station, a park, and a library before the remaining motels banded together to fight the condemnations.

Proposed redevelopment plans stalled in 2002 and 2003; the Stars was demolished around 2006, and the Lincoln was torn down in 2007. Nine motels remain.

The Summit Motel's name comes from its location—a barely-there Chicago hill. It's much easier to see the Summit's resemblance to another Arthur P. Salk-designed motel—downtown's Ohio House.

These days, the shabby exteriors are more of an issue than legal troubles, according to Tim Czarnecki of Alderman O'Connor's office. Promising developments stalled in 2008 with the recession, even with lots that still offer a $500,000 development incentive from the city. Courtesy of Joni Hirsch Blackman

The new police station has helped, and the once-common arrests in the area ranging from possession of drugs to domestic battery, prostitution, and rape, have declined. The motels that remain are more rick-rack than a row, but they're still leaving the lights on, some sixty years later.

NOW IT'S ...

Was: Motel Row

Is: Police station, library, park, and bike path ... and motels

Location: Lincoln Avenue between Foster and Peterson

Tip: The neon sign of 1956's Stars Motel, 6100 N Lincoln Ave., auctioned on eBay after demolition, was never claimed, but was finally removed after years presiding over an empty lot.

Does It Still Have That New Car Smell?

It's the lesser-known Michigan Avenue Street wall: continuous masonry fronts of former automobile showrooms from the earliest days of horseless carriages. Henry Ford was the second, in 1905, to open a showroom there, his first outside of Detroit. The dealership was located on one of Chicago's first fully paved streets, which was perfectly flat for test drives. Just three years earlier, there were only six hundred cars in the entire Chicagoland area. During the next thirty years, however, many of the ninety thousand Chicagoland cars were purchased on Motor Row, the retail district of automobile dealerships housed in multi-story buildings as beautiful as the cars, and designed by architects who were also behind some of the Loop's most famous skyscrapers.

A 1910 *Tribune* special section for the Chicago Automobile Show called it "the most imposing automobile row of any city in the country, and claim for a world's record might well be made without much chance of there being any dispute."

No assembly-line-like set of identical buildings, these historic masterpieces reminiscent of turn-of-the-century movie palaces range from basic two-story to multi-story buildings. Some simply displayed new autos and accessories; others were topped by floors for repair, painting and storage—most 180-feet deep for easy drive-in. Though the cars are long gone, driven after the Depression to suburban expanses of outdoor lots, the remnants of grandeur remain in stone: Medallions still preside above the former showroom windows with names and/or initials of automakers like Pierce, Peerless, Buick, Marmon, Locomobile and Hudson.

In the late 1990s, when the South Loop began to awaken from a long lull, Motor Row found new life as a residential area. Fifty-six buildings were included in the 2001 Motor Row Landmark District. Many have

Up to 116 different makes of cars were sold and repaired in 56 Near-South Side buildings, the largest early motor row in the U.S. still standing.

As noted on the "Motor Row" district sign in the area, "In the early twentieth century, South Michigan Avenue was the heart of splendor in regards to homes, wealth, worship, leisure, and shopping." Elaborate "palace-like" auto showrooms targeted those residents. Courtesy of Illinois Historic Preservation Agency

Inset: The former B.F.Goodrich Co. building, 1925 S Michigan Ave., constructed in 1911 and designed by Christian Eckstrom is one of the most decorative buildings in the district. Courtesy of Illinois Historic Preservation Agency

been turned into lofts—there's a microbrewery, an event space, and plans for more entertainment and residential renovation just outside McCormick Place.

NOW IT'S...

Was: Motor Row

Is: Restaurants, Condos, Bars, Event Spaces, Apartments

Location: South Michigan Ave. between 14th and 25th Sts., along Indiana Ave, (about 2200-3500 South), a few on Wabash in that area

Henry Ford's showroom: An investment made with only $243 remaining in his bank account—the repurposed original building still stands at 1444 S Michigan Ave. Ford later moved to 2229 S Michigan.

Studebaker showroom: 2012-36 S Michigan, now Windy City multifamily units.

Motor Row Brewing, 2337 S Michigan Ave., Motor Row Brewing revived the former Federal Motor Car Co. showroom that was built in 1910. The three-story restored building is now used as a microbrewery with a bar on the ground floor and an office above.

Motor Row Condominiums, 2300 S Michigan Ave., and 2100: a 40-unit loft conversion and 180-unit condo high-rise located at 2100 S Indiana Ave.

Locomobile Lofts, 2000 S Michigan: The quintessential early auto facility still displays the name of the company "Locomobile," for which it was built in 1909 and occupied as a showroom until 1929. This was one of the first loft conversions in Motor Row in 2004.

Marmon Grand Banquet: Former Marmon Co. Showroom at 2232 S Michigan, 1922, "Marmon" still proudly emblazoned on its terra cotta facade.

Motor Row Lofts, former Cadillac and Saxon automobile showrooms, 2301-2312 S Michigan, 1911-1915: Combines three adjacent buildings into one residential complex.

Revel Motor Row event space (opening 2017): Creative use of the 1930s home of the Chicago Illinois Automobile Club and Chicago Defender newspaper.

The former Hudson showroom is renovated in the South Loop neighborhood now known as McCormick Square, south of McCormick Place. Courtesy of Illinois Historic Preservation Agency

The 1936 Philip Maher-designed building, previous home of the Illinois Motor Club and the Chicago Defender newspaper, is now Revel Motor Row event space. The adjacent building, home to the city's first Cadillac dealership at 2412 S Michigan, is part of the new entertainment venue. Courtesy of Illinois Historic Preservation Agency

World's Longest Pier

On July 4, 1916, Chicagoans tried out the brand-new Municipal Pier. "One of the biggest crowds ever assembled in the city," noted the *Tribune*. Many of the fifty thousand visitors lingered past dark "to see Chicago's shore line at night."

Construction began in April 1914, and the cost was $4.5 million. The mission? Business and pleasure—freight and passenger dockage plus recreation.

Early years' summer entertainment included pageants, festivals, concerts, and a child's paradise "with athletic slides, teeter-totters, merry-go-rounds, lawn swings, sand boxes, tables for games."

During World War I, the pier housed barracks for recruits. In 1927, it was renamed Navy Pier to honor WWI Navy personnel. During WWII, more than seventeen thousand Naval air pilots were trained at the pier (including former President George H.W. Bush). Many misdirected WWII planes remain on Lake Michigan's bottom, though several— including one hanging at Midway Airport—have been raised and restored.

Post war, the University of Illinois operated a branch on the pier, nicknamed Harvard on the Rocks. In 1965, the school relocated to the West Loop.

Meanwhile, the Port of Chicago thrived, one of the world's greatest inland ports. The pier was the site of trade shows, social events, circuses, and shipping through the 1960s, particularly after a 1967 fire destroyed the original McCormick Place. When that facility was reopened, Navy Pier sat abandoned for two decades.

A $150 million renovation brought Navy Pier back to its original vision as a commercial and recreational urban playground. The headhouse, towers, and banquet hall at the far end were restored. Opening in 1995

Reported in the *Tribune* in 1916: Municipal Pier gives Chicagoans "a place to go out into the lake, away from the shore a sufficient distance to get away from the city noises and annoyances."

To avoid attacks from coastline submarines, Aircraft Carrier Qualification training was conducted in Lake Michigan, where World War II pilots proved their ability to land and take off from aircraft carriers. Courtesy of Heroes on Deck

Inset: The USS Wilmette was on training duty at Navy Pier from 1942 until the end of World War II. Courtesy of Heroes on Deck

NOW IT'S...

Was: Municipal Pier

Is: Navy Pier - with 2016's 100th anniversary Ferris Wheel 2.0

Location: 600 E Grand Ave.

Tip: Fireworks explode Wednesday and Saturday nights from Memorial Day to Labor Day—a tradition that began with Chicago's 1921 Pageant of Progress pyrotechnics.

with the Shakespeare Theater, shops, restaurants, exhibition facilities, and a Ferris Wheel, it quickly became the number one tourist attraction in the state—apparently, a long walk on a long pier is a timeless paradise.

Yacht Clubbers' Ice-Breaker

The MV *Abegweit* ferried railroad cars, automobiles, and people across the Abegweit Passage of the Northumberland Strait, connecting Port Borden, Prince Edward Island to Cast Tormentine, New Brunswick, from 1947 to 1982. Locals nicknamed the Canadian National Marine's 372-foot ferry the "*Abby*."

In 1982, the *Abby* suffered the equivalent of being put out to pasture—sent to dry dock in Pictou, Nova Scotia with a 'For Sale' sign. Later that year, Chicago's Columbia Yacht Club, in need of a replacement for its too-small 215-feet, 100-year-old Great Lakes Steamer, found, bought, and saved her.

So how does one bring home a 6,692-ton ferry? By sending a sixty-member crew to spend ten twenty-four-hour days navigating her 2,170 miles down the St. Lawrence Seaway, naturally.

The Club's first floating clubhouse took to the harbor in 1892 when founding members built a one-room shed on a thirty-five-foot barge, replacing it with a larger barge. Later, a two-story floating structure the club constructed in 1902 had a ballroom, but lasted only until World War I's toll on members' finances caused its anchor to be pulled up.

By 1925, a new Club Ship—a 193-foot wood and iron-plated steamboat named the *Pere Marquette*—arrived. She, too, was replaced. A 213-foot former side-wheel excursion steamer, the SS *Florida*, anchored here in 1937 and managed to survive the 1955 fire that sunk it. Raised and restored, the SS *Florida* continued clubbing another thirty years. But on April 14, 1983, the MV *Abegweit* arrived in Monroe Harbor, serving admirably.

"*Abby*," strangely, has four propellers—two up front, another two on the stern—for two reasons: to make stern-first port entry easier for a ferry and to chop ice from the bottom up.

The private yacht club's facilities include a dining room, outdoor deck, steering room and lower level, which, when the Abby was a ferry boat, once held automobiles and railcars. Courtesy of Columbia Yacht Club

Inset: In 1983, the 61-foot-wide "Abby," which extends 18 feet below the water surface, pulled into its new home near Lake Point Tower for a fun-filled retirement. Courtesy of Columbia Yacht Club

The former ferry that was capable of cutting through nineteen feet of loose ice or three feet of solid ice now just as ably carries plenty of drink-ready ice cubes, and everything that comes along with them.

NOW IT'S . . .

Was: MV *Abegweit* Ferry

Is: Columbia, home of the Columbia Yacht Club

Location: 111 North Lake Shore Drive (Where East Randolph hits Lake Michigan)

Tip: In 1947, the MV *Abegweit* —meaning "cradled on the waves"—was the heaviest Canadian-built vessel and the world's most powerful icebreaker.

Skyscraper Daddy's Legacy

Famed architect and engineer William Le Baron Jenney's pioneering Home Insurance Building, constructed in 1885, was torn down in 1931. The same fate almost befell this, his New York Life building. Instead, this early-metal-frame-construction gem designed by the "father of the skyscraper" has been beautifully refurbished a a hotel.

Construction began during 1893's World's Columbian Exhibition, and the twelve-story building was completed by the following April. Illustrating just how old that is . . . a story in the February 1894 *Tribune* describes tests given to the building's elevators that "contain several new improvements for the safety and comfort of passengers . . . To test the speed and capacity, three thousand pounds of iron were loaded in the car, with six heavy men, making the load, at the most conservative estimate four thousand pounds."

Another story described "exterior walls of the first three floors are of light gray granite and above this they are entirely of a light gray terra cotta." Though then known as the New York Life building, it's no wonder it is now the Gray Hotel.

Not much has changed since the 120-year-old story proclaimed "the building in all its appointments is of the best." The New York Life insurance company's Midwest headquarters occupied the entire third floor; the 11th was home to Hartford Insurance. Additional floors were added in 1898 and 1902, making fourteen in all.

Half of the historic structure was nearly torn down in 2006 to make way for a hotel and office tower next door, but preservationists' outrage was unrelenting. Kimpton Hotels bought the Financial District building in 2014 and the hotel opened two years later with a top-floor ballroom, and a sunny (not gray) forecast.

New York Life was on Preservation Chicago's 2006 list of most threatened buildings, calling it "the closest link with the ground-breaking technology of Jenney's Home Insurance Building."

The $106 million conversion of the 1894 structure was completed in 2016 consisting of 281 hotel rooms, a restaurant and bar, meeting and event space. Courtesy of Library of Congress

Inset: The second-floor lobby bar, "Volume 39," honors the old law books from law firms that once inhabited the building, as well as the 39 South LaSalle address. Courtesy of Kimpton Hotels

NOW IT'S...

Was: The New York Life Insurance Building

Is: The Kimpton Gray Hotel

Location: 39 S LaSalle St. and 122 W Monroe St.

Tip: The 14th floor retractable-roof Boleo bar offers a peek of Jenney's famed riveted steel columns.

At the Six Corners of Yesterday and Today

Founded in Chicago in 1901, it's appropriate that Walgreen's helped save the life of a 1921 city landmark—Noel State Bank. Bank founder Joseph R. Noel was a physician who hung up his stethoscope in 1897 to manage his father's business, Noel Proprietary Medicine Co. Theophilus Noel made a fortune manufacturing something he called "Vitae-ore." (The government later dubbed it "snake oil.")

Doc Noel invested in Wicker Park's North West Savings Bank in 1905, which in 1917 became Noel State Bank. Gardner C. Coughlen designed the new bank, completed in 1919. But the Noel name didn't reign on the flatiron-shaped beauty long, succumbing to a bank run of $4 million in 1931.

Later a Fairfield Savings and Loan, then Midwest Bank, it was empty as of 2005. Restoration from March 2010 to June 2012 unveiled a newly landmarked flagship Walgreens. Dozens of bits of history were preserved, referenced, and restored as the building's past is wholeheartedly celebrated in this gem of adaptive reuse.

At the November 2012 grand opening, customers and politicians marveled over the original elements that had been refurbished: the tile floor, iron ventilation grates, pendant light fixture, and a huge skylight, which had been intact but needed to be removed piece by piece, cleaned and replaced. Surrounding the skylight are dozens of hexagonal ceiling trays and the building's coffered ceiling features a large stained glass window with a similar six-point star design.

The former bank vault in the corner of the lower level pharmacy department showcases historic Walgreens artifacts, including original apothecary implements and vessels.

On the exterior, the store is identified by a simple, large "W," designed

The bank's original cast iron safe is now a "vitamin vault"—vitamins and supplements alongside safe deposit boxes showcasing historic Walgreens products.

vitamin vault

Alderman Scott Waguespack, whose grandfather was a Noel Bank customer, wanting to avoid the bitter pill of " a really bad gut rehab," instead encouraged Walgreens' restoration—so breathtaking, it can cure ails better than Theo's potions. Courtesy of Diane Miskiewicz

Inset: Customers can bank on feeling better just walking in. Pause in the vestibule to see a photo of the old Noel State Bank's interior. Courtesy of Jone Hirsch Blackman

so no building details are hidden. The curved mechanical sliding glass entry doors are only the second such set in the world—the others are Taser's company headquarters. Talk about an intersection of old and new.

NOW IT'S...

Was: Noel State Bank Building

Is: Walgreen's at the corner of North Avenue, Damen Avenue and Milwaukee Avenue.

Location: 1601 N Milwaukee Avenue

Tip: This 24-hour Walgreens has a small parking lot and an entry door in the back.

Don't Blame the Cow

For more than a century, her cow was blamed for the fire that started on a dry October night in 1871. The famous blaze was carried east, then north by Chicago winds—away from Catherine O'Leary's home, but throughout the downtown that had been constructed mostly with wood. A day and a half later, one hundred thousand people were left homeless, three hundred had died, and three square miles from the near south side north to about Fullerton Avenue was left smoldering.

O'Leary and husband Patrick's land now holds a most appropriate monument of sorts—since 1961, thereupon sits the Chicago Fire Department's training academy.

But the mystery of the great fire's cause outlived their barn. In 1871, O'Leary told investigators she never milked at night. She pointed to partying tenants who may have milking cows. Others were also suspected—neighbor Daniel "Peg Leg" Sullivan was first on the scene (despite his wooden leg.) He accused O'Leary. O'Leary's son and other boys shooting dice in the hayloft were also implicated.

The commission never came to a conclusion, yet the tale of Mrs. O'Leary milking the cow who kicked a lantern into the hay persisted for more than a century. In 1937, the Historical Society erected a plaque: "On this site stood home and barn of Mrs. O'Leary where the Chicago fire of 1871 started. Although there are many versions of the story of its origin, the real cause of the fire has never been determined."

The $2 million fire academy's construction, then the most comprehensive fire training school ever built, has sparked happier connections to the site.

Thirty-six years later, the city council's Committee of Fire and Police reconsidered the cow's culpability. Historians using transcripts from the old fire inquiry hearings and contemporary tract records believed eyewitness Sullivan couldn't have had a clear view of the barn from a neighbor's

"Mrs. Kate O'Leary and her cow are innocent of any blame for the fire that raged behind their house," declared Alderman Ed Burke in his 1997 City Council resolution.

"Almost everything in the path of the fire had been destroyed" in the thirty hours that the Great Fire burned in October 1871. This photo was labeled "Mrs. O'Leary's residence." Courtesy of Library of Congress

Inset: In February 1961, the Chicago Fire Academy was "a guarantee to Chicago citizens that such a fire would never be repeated," said a *Tribune* article. The Egon Weiner sculpture of a flame, titled *Pillar of Fire*, sits where the Great Fire is believed to have begun. Courtesy of Joni Hirsch Blackman

front stoop. He was the likely culprit, they concluded, while O'Leary was probably asleep in bed.

History's first cow-framing attempt finally put to rest.

NOW IT'S ...

Was: Patrick & Catherine O'Leary house and (their cow's) barn

Is: Chicago Fire Department's Robert J. Quinn Fire Academy

Location: 558 W DeKoven St.

Tip: Free, open weekdays 10 a.m. – 2 p.m.; look for a tile marked "1871"—the spot where the fire began.

From Old-School Skyscraper to New College Dorm

An 1893 newspaper article described the under-construction Old Colony Building:

"It is divided into three stages, the first being the lower three stories, the second being the next eleven, and the third being the fifteenth and sixteenth stories and the attic. The whole is surmounted with a heavily molded and bracketed cornice . . . The building as a whole bears a striking resemblance to a beautiful column with its base, shaft and capital."

Any student of architecture will recognize that textbook Chicago architectural organization, the classic "tripartite" design of the day. The recurring template meant "solid" to residents afraid of new, potentially shaky skyscrapers.

"Old Colony" is carved above the elaborate Dearborn doorway, "one of the most imposing in the city."

Most amusing is the description of the white terra-cotta paving bricks used for the structure's upper stories: "It is expected that Chicago smoke will soil them, though they are too hard to absorb soot to any extent. It is designed to scrub the building off every year or two, so that it will constantly appear something like white marble."

Ah, best laid plans . . . for years, until a 2015 renovation, the Old Colony looked nearly black.

The 1894 building's Boston owner named it for Massachusett's first English colony, featuring the seal of Plymouth colony on either side of the exterior entrance and on interior elevators.

Deemed the "most completely fire-proofed building" in America by a Russian professor studying the subject, it was one of the early metal frame

"The Arc at Old Colony," apartments are marketed to South Loop college students. The name is an homage to the innovative, arched "portal braces" that buttressed its internal metal frame against Chicago wind.

It's easy to tell when this undated photo was taken since the "L" tracks were built three years after the Old Colony was constructed in 1894. Courtesy of Library of Congress

Inset: The $35 million rehab/facade restoration in 2015 converted the old office building to a dorm-like apartment complex. The study lounge on the second floor celebrates the Holabird & Roche building's impressive past.Courtesy of ARC @Old Colony

buildings. It was designed for three hundred to five hundred newfangled offices equipped with telephones and elevators upstairs with and a two-story bank below.

Easy to identify by its rounded "oriel" window bays at the corners, those are now unusual, desirable living spaces overlooking the Loop. Many turn-of-the-century building features—the Tiffany mosaic floors, marble wainscoting, and ornate elevator details—remain. Residents, however, are strictly circa turn-of-the-next-century.

NOW IT'S...

Was: Old Colony office building

Is: The Arc at Old Colony (dorm-style apartments)

Location: 37 W Van Buren St.

Tip: Previously hidden two-story Van Buren entrance with columns is restored, still partially obscured by the later-constructed "L" tracks.

Virgin Furs

The world's first Virgin Hotel can't get any farther from the photo in the 1927 *Chicago Tribune* when Old Dearborn Bank opened: several stone-faced long-time Chicagoans standing in front of an 1803 Fort Dearborn cannon and a replica of the fort's log cabin—all on exhibit at the brand-new bank building.

The bank's heritage went back 124 years earlier, when furs were used in lieu of money to trade with friendly Native Americans. The structure was constructed on land once occupied by a fur company headquartered in a log cabin once owned by the government because it was on the Fort Dearborn property.

Old Dearborn Bank took the name upon moving into the new building—formerly the Lake-State bank. Old Dearborn's first chairman was Kraft cheese scion James Kraft.

One of two office buildings designed by movie palace architects C. W. and George Rapp, the brick skyscraper's unusual figures carved into the base and capital reflected the spirit of the 1920s.

The bank didn't celebrate the era for long—it was taken over a year or so after the move, but then that bank liquidated during the Great Depression. The office building has endured, but by the time it was sold to Virgin Hotels in 2011, few offices were occupied.

British billionaire Richard Branson's "first urban hotel" opened in January 2015 following a well-received refurbishment. The company kept its promise to retain many of the unique features of the property they "fell in love with."

On the exterior, "a virtual menagerie of animals (some real, some mythological) ...Lions, birds, griffins and squirrels—the latter symbolizing humans squirreling away their savings," wrote Blair Kamin, *Tribune* architecture critic.

An early photo of the two-story banking hall featuring the elevators' brass doors, which have been richly restored. Courtesy of Ryerson and Burnham Archives, The Art Institute of Chicago

Inset: An under-construction view of the 1928 building. Note the canopy toward the lower center, where the Virgin Hotel sign now hangs, and the distinctive relief sculptures above the second-floor windows. Courtesy of Ryerson and Burnham Archives, The Art Institute of Chicago

A canopy over the sidewalk topped with a red "Virgin" sign marks the 250-room hotel. Inside the front door, the original cigar bar acts as a front desk. A limestone and oak staircase (with a pop of Virgin-red carpet) and bronze elevator doors ooze "old Chicago," while upstairs a bar, restaurant, coffee shop, library and laptop/hang-out areas have a more twenty-first-century vibe.

NOW IT'S...

Was: Old Dearborn Bank

Is: Virgin Hotel

Location: 203 N Wabash Ave.

Tip: Along with the exquisite animal carvings on the exterior, various birds are depicted on the ornate bronze grills in the entry vestibule.

A Small Coffee (page 138): You can lead a student to coffee . . . and they'll drink, even if there's no seating inside the shop.

—Courtesy of Joni Hirsch Blackman

Jazzy Mural (page 182): Up a few stairs at the back of the Meyers Ace Hardware store was a small, cramped office with this bold mural on the wall, apparently painted in the 1950s by a local bassist, Richard Evans, who also worked at Chess Records.

—Courtesy of Joni Hirsch Blackman

The Old Central Post office (page 24): In the Batman movie The Dark Knight it was both the Gotham Police headquarters and Gotham National Bank. In Transformers: Dark of the Moon, the old Chicago Post Office's east facade was decorated as the "Department of Health and Human Services." In real life, it has been abandoned and deteriorating since 1996. Renovation began in 2016, a few months before this photo.

—Courtesy of Joni Hirsch Blackman

Post Office Lobby (page 24): The inside of the grand old Art Deco post office hasn't been seen by the public since 1996, but 601W Companies developers are restoring the 2.5 million square foot building to its former opulence with an expected 2020 opening.

—Courtesy of Urban Remains.

AKA Aldine Hall (page 184): After the Old Town School of Folk Music moved to Lincoln Avenue in 1998, their previous main office on Armitage, AKA Aldine hall, was kept for the school's children's programming.

—Courtesy of Paul Hirsch Photography

Morrie Mages (page 49): A 1970s photo of 620 N Lasalle when Morrie Mages Sports had recently moved to the former coffee warehouse.

—Courtesy of Lili Ann Mages Zisook

The Sports Authority (page 49): In 2017, the Sports Authority had moved out and the building was slated to be either torn down or renovated, but Morrie Mages' famously numbered floors remained.

—Courtesy of Joni Hirsch Blackman

Chicago Cultural Center's Palatial Interior (page 22): From the Preston Bradley room plaque: "Since the morning of Oct. 11,1897, this spectacular room has served visitors in pursuit of inspiration, information and enlightenment. Originally designed as the place where the Chicago Public Library's extensive volumes were delivered to patrons, this extravagant space, named for the distinguished clergyman and library board member Dr. Reverend Preston Bradley, has served in recent decades as a venue for the performing arts, public conversations and civic celebrations."

—Courtesy of Gia Dragoi Photography

Home Bank Vault in The Bedford (page 70): The former bank vault with safe deposit boxes is used as the Bedford lounge or available for private events, while just outside the vault is the Bedford's dining room, set up here for a private event.

—Courtesy of The Bedford Bar/Restaurant

Hampton Inn's Art Deco Lobby (page 32): A 1929 Chicago Motor Club ad says, "A lobby different from anything you have ever seen—done in an original art moderne motif. As you enter, sensations of richness and spaciousness vie with each other." Truly, not much has changed.

—Courtesy of Hampton Inn Downtown Chicago/North Loop

2017 Wolf Point (page 204): The formerly ignored and abhorred Chicago River is now lined with grand residential and office towers—clearly obvious here at Wolf Point, in 2017.

—Courtesy of Joni Hirsch Blackman

1989 Wolf Point (page 204): The same location on the Chicago River—Wolf Point—nearly 30 years earlier. This 1989 view has very little in common with today's sparkling river other than Fulton House on the far right with its distinctive circular windows near the top of the brick former warehouse.

—Courtesy of William Brubaker

Trains Before Millennium Park Beauty (page 72): This 1968 view shows the type of scene Mayor Richard M. Daley saw when he first imagined this could be (an incredibly expensive yet cherished) future park.

—Courtesy of William Brubaker

Pre-East Bank Club (page 148): Long before there was an East Bank Club, the Kinzie Street terminal was the end of the line for the Chicago & Evanston and the Chicago & Pacific railways.

Hidden Loop Staple Once Housed a Stable

Every day, Chicagoans walk past a nine-foot-wide alley on Jackson Boulevard between State Street and Wabash Avenue, missing one of the Loop's oldest and smallest buildings. Tightly wedged between two skyscrapers, the three-story, nineteen-by-nineteen-foot brick structure at the alley's dead end is invisible to those who—perhaps because they haven't yet had their coffee?—don't peer closer.

It has been inaccurately said to have survived the Great Chicago Fire of 1871. Actually, this building was constructed on "the stable lot" several years after the Pickwick Stable, built around 1857, was destroyed by the fire. Grocer/flour merchant Henry Horner, whose namesake grandson became an Illinois governor, was the owner. The "new" two-story building was topped with a third story in 1892, so William and Fannie Abson could live above their restaurant, Col. Abson's Chop House. Skyscrapers later constructed on either side didn't just hem the building in, they made it disappear from view—even on satellite and aerial photos.

In the twentieth century, various taverns moved to Pickwick Place (now Pickwick Lane): Red Path Inn, Robinson's, the Pickwick, and 22 East, which was described in the June 14, 1947 *Chicago Tribune*: "On the ground floor is the bar, dark and quiet with black beamed ceiling, casement windows, old beer steins, and two or three tables for the fastidious. Out of it rises a precarious winding staircase to a tiny dining room large enough for only seven round oak tables. On the third floor is the kitchen, presided over by a mother and daughter team who have been there so long the patrons call them by their first names, Freda and Mitzi. The three floors are connected by an ancient dumbwaiter."

"One of the quietest little retreats in the Loop, as anachronistic to its setting as Loop pigeons. It is shadowy, removed, and something like a library reading room," 1947 Tribune.

After the Pickwick Stables burned down in the Great Fire of 1871, this brick structure took its place—nearly as small as a stable, but filled with much better food. Courtesy of Pickwick Roasters

Customers were mostly local, working in the area's clothing trade. "The average Loop habitué don't know it exists," Marcia Winn's column concluded—a statement still true more than seventy years later.

Asado Coffee spent a couple of years in the space. Pickwick Coffee Roasting Company opened there in 2016 with a neigh to the past: a horse head logo. The space is now occupied by Hero Coffee Roasters.

NOW IT'S ...

Was: Pickwick Stable/Colonel Abson's Chop House

Is: Hero Coffee Roasters

Location: 22 E Jackson Blvd.

Tip: Nearly torn down in the 1970s, the alley entrance to 22 East was blocked by steel gates in 1897 and 2013, making the building inaccessible.

Cleanliness, then Dirtiness

One of the country's finest Art Deco towers, 1929's Palmolive Building, was the first commercial skyscraper built far from the Loop at the north end of Michigan Avenue, across from the Drake hotel, in an area where apartments and upscale shops had reigned.

Architects Holabird & Root designed it for one of the largest soap manufacturers in the world, hence the *Chicago Tribune*'s description: "a monument to cleanliness." Atop the Palmolive roof was placed "the world's biggest light . . . with a rating of two billion candlepower, visible to aviators in the air three hundred miles away."

The Lindbergh Beacon was fitted with an aluminum shield in 1969, to keep one area of the revolving beam from shining into the new John Hancock Building's condo windows. In 1981, it was removed completely after residents living in the many skyscrapers then surrounding the 37-story tower complained. In 2007, a softer eighteen-thousand-watt light was installed toward the north in an arc over Lake Michigan.

The building kept the Palmolive name even after the soap firm moved to New York in 1934. On leap day 1960, a new tenant moved to the first floor, drawing more than 132,000 curious guests in the first three months—the busiest club in the world. The attraction was its waitresses dressed as bunnies, each complete with ears and a cotton tail.

A Rabbit-headed metal Playboy key allowed members past the door Bunny into the world's first Playboy Club. Five years later, Hugh Hefner's company leased nine floors, and by 1968, PLAYBOY was illuminated atop the former Palmolive in nine-foot-tall letters. Twenty years later, Playboy moved to smaller offices on Lake Shore Drive. The art deco icon became the Palmolive again in 2002, converted to 103 condominiums . . . with a different sort of beacon: an enlightened century.

"When we were kids, we could see that beacon sweeping across the sky at night . . . I think that's the reason that building eventually became the Playboy Building."
—Hugh Hefner

Once the home of the Colgate-Palmolive-Peet Company, again named The Palmolive Building. But the retail and office portion of the building is known as 919 N Michigan. Courtesy of Curt Teich Co.

Inset: The Lindbergh beacon was the world's biggest light, hung on a 135-foot standard, the beacon flashed a "welcome" from 603 feet up.

NOW IT'S...

Was: The Palmolive Building, then the Playboy Building

Is: The Palmolive Building

Location: 919 N Michigan Ave.

Tip: Look up when near first-floor retail. Residents —for ten years that included actor Vince Vaughn—use the art deco setbacks as patios.

61

Police Playhouse

The Chicago Children's Theater sign on the building at Racine and Monroe is somewhat transparent, allowing passersby to see the letters that were carved into the building's stone many years ago: "Police Station."

"Ground-breaking" in December 2015 featured children wearing an array of colored construction helmets to celebrate their theater's new home. It had been staging productions for ten years at various museums, theaters, and other venues around the city and suburbs. This, for the first time, is their own dedicated space.

"It was a vacant building yesterday," Deputy Mayor Steve Koch said at the ceremony. "It's a vacant building today. But tomorrow, we're going to fill it with opportunity, and it's going to be an incredible place."

An optimistic future for a building that spent sixty-four years on generally grimmer business—business of which remnants linger: Bars remain on some windows.

The 149-seat Pritzker Family Studio Theater is where the station's cell block was located. The basement of the 1948 building had a gun range for officers.

Since March 2017 it has been filled with happy pursuits: classrooms for camps and workshops, as well as an informal lobby waiting room for students and parents. The Red Kite interactive theater is dedicated to kids with autism, a program pioneered by CCT, which also offers programs for children with impaired vision or hearing and Down's syndrome.

The Station renovation is owed partly to a $5 million Illinois Department of Commerce and Economic Opportunity grant received in 2014. Then-governor Pat Quinn's office said it was part of his agenda to "provide educational and artistic opportunities for all Illinois children." Standing ovation earned.

"We do not want either the children, their parents, or this community to forget the history of this building," said Frank Maugeri, artistic director.

This 1948 building, designed by Paul Gerhardt., Jr., was converted into a children's theater—a project that garnered calls of support from both the mayor and governor's offices. Courtesy of Wheeler Kearns Architects

Inset: The old jail cells are gone; in their place is now the 149-seat Pritzker Family Studio Theater. Courtesy of Wheeler Kearns Architects

NOW IT'S...

Was: 12th District Chicago Police station

Is: Chicago Children's Theater

Location: 100 S Racine Ave.

Tip: The non-profit, Equity-affiliated theater company is devoted exclusively to young audiences. Tickets at chicagochildrenstheater.org.

62

When Words Needed Paper

In the late 1800s, Chicago became home to the brand-new mail order industry. Aaron Montgomery Ward invented it; Sears, Roebuck enlarged it. They, as well as Spiegel and other local businesses, needed presses to print their catalogs. Publishers of things like phone directories, maps, and books needed printers too.

After the Great Fire of 1871, the city redeveloped into various districts— shopping, banking, cultural, and, in the particular area with long, narrow blocks offering thin lots, printing. Everything the typesetters and engravers needed was here: a train station to bring workers in and take products out; narrow streets—requiring narrower buildings with windows on each side—for maximum light in the buildings.

The buildings were designed by many of the city's most prominent architects, leaving this district with printing houses and office buildings as impressive as the words printed within.

The area thrived for years, but gradually, various pressures converged— photo offset printing replaced letterpress; new heavier presses caused printers to move to one-story concrete buildings; the once-advantageous narrow streets were difficult for trucks to navigate, and airline travel eventually caused Dearborn Street Station to close. Printers moved to the suburbs, the Congress Expressway opened nearby, and by the 1960s, Printer's Row was mostly vacant. Late 1970, several buildings were converted to lofts.

Printing House Row structures include:

The Donohue building, 711 and 727 S Dearborn St., architects Julius Speyuer and Alfred Alschuler in 1883 and 1913—Built around the same time as Dearborn Street Station, the presses were in the basement, street-level spaces were rented to shops, and the upper floors were publishing company offices. Bookbinding was done on the eighth floor where the natural light was best.

Lakeside Press Building, 731 S Plymouth Ct., architect Howard Van Doren Shaw, 1897 (south section) and 1901 (north addition)—Owned by R.R. Donnelley, printers of various directories. Showrooms were eon the first floor, offices on the second and printing above.

Since 1883, Printers Row employed immigrants in publishing houses as typesetters, etchers, mapmakers, and bookbinders at places like Rand McNally and R. R. Donnelley

Lakeside Press's logo, an Indian head over Fort Dearborn, is in limestone relief over the building's main entrance here in 1963. Courtesy of Library of Congress

New Franklin Building, 718-736 S Dearborn St., George Nimmons, 1912—On the front of the building, colored tiles depict men at work on early printing presses; at the top, a huge skylight brought in plenty of light to bind books.

The Pontiac Building, 542 S Dearborn St., Holabird and Roche, 1891—The oldest remaining example of this prolific pair of architects, commissioned by the Rooks Brothers of Boston (who commissioned many early Chicago skyscrapers); named after an Ottawa Indian Chief.

The Terminals Building, 537 S Dearborn, John Van Osdel, 1892—An original capping cornice was removed from this building that in the early 1900s housed trade perodicals.

The Transportation Building, 600 S Dearborn, Fred Prather, 1911—Housed railway company offices and other railroad-dependent businesses. It was the tallest in the district at twenty-two stories.

NOW IT'S...

Was: Printing House Row

Is: Printer's Row Historic District

Location: (see above) From Congress Parkway to Polk Street, Plymouth Court to the Chicago River

Tip: Originally known as the Printer's Row Book Fair, the free, outdoor, two-day Printer's Row Lit Fest has been held annually since 1985.

Terminal (with a Target) on the Slip

The six-story red brick warehouse on the north side of Ogden slip (parallel to the north bank of the Chicago River) was constructed between 1905 and 1920 by Chicago Dock and Canal Trust. Seven of the original eighteen sections remain, enough to visualize when the wharves, docks, piers, and slip known as the Pugh Terminal Warehouse were operated by lessee James Pugh.

Pugh realized the city needed a permanent wholesale product exposition center after the 1893 World's Columbian Expedition. With access to rail, ships, and the Chicago Tunnel System, the terminal was perfectly located. Pugh modeled his furniture exhibition and distribution facility after the auto showrooms of Motor Row on South Michigan Avenue. Multiple manufacturers could display furniture under one roof, eliminating buyers' needs to run all over town.

The company suffered soon after Pugh's death in 1925 when the new Merchandise Mart and American Furniture Mart left the terminal with a more limited warehousing role. But the pattern for the "North Pier" or "St. Clair Manufacturing District" neighborhood had been set to lighter industry than warehouses along the Chicago River.

Renovated into retail and commercial space known as North Pier in 1990, it housed a popular mix of restaurants, shops, offices, and a young Chicago Children's Museum. The museum moved in 1995 to Navy Pier and the office and retail building was re-named River East. A loft-condominium conversion was derailed during the Great Recession but, in 2015, The Lofts at River East opened with 285 luxury apartments. Included at the building's corner is a small Target store.

In the history of Chicago's waterfront, Pugh Terminal "is probably the only building left that can ... bring back the flavor of that time, when ... there was this maritime activity," said preservationist Robert Meers.

A 1985 view of North Pier Terminal. Previously Pugh's Furniture Exhibition Company, its more than one hundred acres of floor space was said to be the largest warehouse in the world. Courtesy of C. William Brubaker Collection, University of Illinois at Chicago

Inset: Some believed the entire terminal should have been demolished years ago, but remaining sections are picturesque. Courtesy of David Blachman

Pinstripes—a bowling, bocce, and banquet facility—opened inside, along the water of Ogden Slip, where boaters can dock. One hundred years after its construction, the long building is a striking reminder of the area's industrial past.

NOW IT'S . . .

Was: Pugh Terminal Warehouse, North Pier Terminal

Is: Lofts at River East

Location: 435 E Illinois St. (Lake Shore Drive between the Ogden Slip and Illinois)

Tip: Tilting Pugh Terminal upright would make it one of the tallest buildings in Streeterville, like "Willis Tower laying on its side."

···

Warehouse with Railway and River!

An item of "unusual importance and significance" was reported in the Feb. 14, 1909 *Chicago Tribune*: the proposed warehouse of the Railway Terminal and Warehouse Company to be constructed with 231 feet of frontage on the Chicago River.

This valentine to the upcoming project continues, "Not only is the project of importance because of its magnitude, involving, together with the land, an investment of over $600,000, but it has a peculiar interest by reason of the fact that it is to prove a bonded warehouse for the oriental business of the Milwaukee and St. Paul road when it has completed its connections with the Pacific coast and also is to take care of the produce from the irrigated districts of the west along the line of that road."

Turning into something like a late-night infomercial, the front-section news item literally adds . . . "But that is not all"! This 283,000-square-foot warehouse also included one of "the lighterage stations of the Chicago Lighterage company." Lighterage, perhaps not as obvious in the 21st century, is the process of transferring cargo between vessels of different sizes.

And more! The building would "have connection with" the Illinois Tunnel company, "certain to make it an important factor in the development of the district in which it is located."

"Six stories and basement, of sprinkled, heavy, mill construction is planned also to put in a new dock eight feet wide along the river frontage, and will have street car service along its Indiana Street frontage."

The red brick, 190-foot-wide building was sold in 1947 for $765,000; two years later it was reconfigured as a printing plant and known as The Wallace Press building. In 1963, the company became Wallace Business Forms.

The wider-than-usual structure's middle was used for bonus storage rooms during its residential conversion, and old machine rooms above elevator shafts were cleverly turned into penthouses.

A 1985 view of the Wallace Press building (later Wallace Business Forms Building, and now River Bank Lofts) and the Grand Avenue bridge. Courtesy of C. William Brubaker Collection, University of Illinois at Chicago

Inset: Twenty years after the residential conversion, the bridge house to its south, one of the earliest bridge house designs, got a new, slanted roof. Courtesy of Joni Hirsch Blackman

Thirty years later, the industrial building was purchased for conversion to 128 condominium lofts. So, though its accolades now include being the earliest warehouse-to-residential conversion in River North, it still does not slice and dice.

NOW IT'S...

Was: Railroad Terminal & Warehouse, Wallace Press Building

Is: River Bank Lofts

Location: 550 N Kingsbury St.

Tip: Residential conversion was completed in 1995, before the city's public riverwalk access requirement, so west side units have private riverfront decks.

Living, Dying, and Investing on Erie

When construction of the stone mansion began in 1885, it was surrounded by residences belonging to the well-heeled families whose names populated newspaper society columns. One of the few remaining area homes, this striking turreted structure was designed by Cobb & Frost for Ransom R. Cable, president of the Chicago, Rock Island, and Pacific Railway Company from 1883 to 1898.

Cable had paid $110,000 for the house, but sold it in 1907 after "several negotiations during the last two or three years" to R. Hall McCormick, for his son, assistant state's attorney Robert H. McCormick, for $27,500.

By at least 1936, it was used as the residence of a Northwestern University medical fraternity, Nu Sigma Nu. Dr. George Irwin remembers living on the third floor as a freshman during the winter of 1939-40, before Northwestern offered housing. "Meals were prepared in the basement and served in the ornate dining room; a dumbwaiter brought food up," said Irwin, who paid $25 a month for room and board. His fond memories of the immense house include "evidence of it having been very fancy: parquet floors, mahogany shelves, a music room with piano, gorgeous moulding—it was a sight to behold."

Sixteen students slept on the third floor in bunks, Irwin remembered. "It was a little short on bathrooms as you might expect from the 1890s, but there was running water on all three floors."

Sold to brothers Eugene and John Carroll (John Carroll Sons undertakers) for $43,000 in 1941, it remained a funeral home for fifty years, amassing an impressive roster of luminaries whose final moments above ground were spent there. (Years earlier, the brothers' father, John Carroll,

The bodies of many famous citizens rested in this building. Eugene J. Carroll once said: "We've buried a president, three cardinals, and dozens of mayors and members of the clergy."

Dr. George Irwin and his roommate had the third-floor room on the southeast corner, which shared a bath with the adjoining room, occupied by two other freshmen. Courtesy of Cornell University Library

drove the horse-drawn hearse carrying the body of President Abraham Lincoln through Chicago and into Springfield.)

Renovations began in 1991 to convert it into the headquarters of Driehaus Capital Management, owned by preservationist and philanthropist Richard Driehaus. From death to tax-deferred?

NOW IT'S...

Was: Ransom Cable House, Robert H. McCormick home, John Carroll & Sons Funeral Home

Is: Driehaus Capital Management

Location: 25 E Erie St.

Tip: The building's interior is closed to the public, but no original features remain. The easily-viewed exterior is beautifully restored.

"Building B. Goode"

Like Beyonce or Elvis, this building is commonly known by half of the usual identifier: simply 2120.

International tourists show up just to take a photo next to those four numbers on the doorway. Without the numerals, the typical 1950s storefront would be unrecognizable as a legendary recording studio.

Behind the unassuming doorway, from 1957 to 1967 "some of the most influential recordings in the creative development of the blues and Rock 'n' Roll" were produced, according to the building's landmark designation nomination.

Chess Records was one of several studios comprising South Michigan Avenue's Record Row (between Roosevelt and 22nd Street)—including Curtom Records, Vee-Jay Records, Brunswick Records, King Records, and United Distributors. Chess moved to the light industrial loft neighborhood in 1957. Many recording and record distributing companies located there (some moving from an earlier "Record Row" on Cottage Grove Avenue between 47th and 50th Streets.) The two-story 1911 building was built for an automobile parts sales company—later it housed a slipcover manufacturer and a necktie firm; they remodeled it for offices, shipping facilities, and—this was key—a first-class second-floor recording studio. From there, countless important blues and rock singles and albums were produced and released.

South Side nightclub owners Leonard and Phil Chess, sons of immigrant parents, recognized the potential of the musicians who played in their clubs and wanted to give their music a wider audience.

What the brothers lacked in blues knowledge, they made up for in nightclub experience—they followed those gut instincts, encouraging emotional spontaneity in their artists that others had stifled in recordings.

The brothers hired composer Willie Dixon, a Mississippi native, to coordinate their studio's recordings. Their stars included Sonny Boy Williamson, J.B. Lenoir, Howlin' Wolf, Little Walter, and Muddy Waters, despite the fact that Leonard Chess reportedly complained, "I can't understand what he's singing."

Two major recording studios were headquartered in the building: Vee Jay Records (1960 – 1966) and Brunswick Records (1966 – 1976). The Four Seasons, Little Richard, Jackie Wilson and John Lee Hooker recorded here. The Beatles' first U.S. album was on the Vee Jay label and distributed here. Courtesy of Illinois Historic Preservation Agency

Inset: In 1911, Horatio Wilson designed this two-story brick building for the sale and storage of automobile parts. In 1957, John S. Townsend, Jr. and Jack S. Wiener remodeled the building for Chess Records. They outfitted the building with a recording studio, executive offices and 50s style colors and "snappy" finishes. Courtesy of Illinois Historic Preservation Agency

Two Chess-discovered artists were future Rock 'n' Rollers Bo Diddley and Chuck Berry. The latter recorded four of his seven top-ten singles at 2120. Chess artists are said to have provided creative inspiration for the Beatles, Eric Clapton, and of course Rolling Stones principals Mick Jagger and Keith Richards, who famously re-established a childhood friendship over their mutual admiration of Chess Records, then known as "America's greatest blues label."

"Greatest," perhaps. But definitely "Goode."

The Rolling Stones recorded "2120 South Michigan Avenue" in 1964 as a tribute to Chess and the music originating from that address. Also recorded here: Chuck Berry's "Johnny B. Goode."

Record distributors were located all along South Michigan Avenue, from the 1300 block to the 2200 block starting in the early 1960s. They include:

Chess Lofts, 320 E 21st. St., former warehouse where Chess artists recorded in the 1960s. It was converted to lofts in 2007.

Vee Jay Records, 1449 S Michigan Ave., which was an early U.S. label of the Beatles. The location was sold to Brunswick Records in 1967.

The Horatio Wilson-designed building and the park next door celebrate the talent developer, songwriter, arranger, and performer integral to the Chess brothers' success. Courtesy of Joni Hirsch Blackman

NOW IT'S...

Was: Chess Records, part of Records Row

Is: Willie Dixon's Blues Heaven Foundation

Location: 2120 S Michigan Ave.

Tip: Dixon's widow, Marie, renovated and re-opened in 1997 as Willie Dixon's Blues Heaven Foundation, where tours are offered. (http://www.bluesheaven.com/home.html)

Throw Eggs at Traffic Court

Scottish immigrants Simon Reid and Thomas Murdoch's Dubuque, Iowa, grocery stores offered provisions for wagon trains on the Oregon Trail as early as 1853. As Chicago became the world's largest railroad center, the young men quickly went east to establish a food distribution center.

Reid-Murdoch & Company became one of the country's largest wholesale grocers. In 1914, they built a new building, perfectly located on the Chicago River. The company could ship and receive goods via steamer on the south side and railroad spurs on the north side, while trucks were loaded from the shipping platform under Lasalle Street—or even through the freight tunnel system sixty feet below street level.

Considered one of the city's best examples of industrial design, it's a reminder of the type of buildings once lining the entire river.

It was the first building to conform to 1909's Plan of Chicago riverfront specifications, with docking facilities recessed at the water level and a promenade at street level. Home to corporate offices and warehouse space, several floors were dedicated to manufacturing and processing cheese, coffee, sugar, fish, and pickles, among other foods.

The building is lopsided. In 1926, the westernmost of the original six bays flanking the distinctive clock tower was removed to accommodate the widening of Lasalle Street. In 1954, then owned by Consolidated Grocers, it was sold to the city of Chicago.

For decades it served, somewhat poorly, as the city's traffic court: "The architect did a great job designing it for a food storage warehouse," a judge once said.

The building's basement and first floor became a temporary hospital and morgue in 1915 when the S.S. *Eastland*, docked across the river, rolled onto its side, killing 844 people.

Note the symmetry of the under-construction structure, which was marred slightly in 1927 when the corner was removed to accommodate LaSalle Street's expansion north. Courtesy of Library of Congress

Inset: The refurbished 1914 Reid-Murdoch Building, with logos of its original owners (lions) at the top of its clock tower. Courtesy of Friedman Properties

Various city departments and agencies remained until 2001, when Friedman Properties restored historic elements and turned it into mixed-use office space. The two-level public riverwalk has outdoor restaurant seating and a water taxi stop. At least this taxi can't get traffic tickets.

NOW IT'S...

Was: Reid, Murdoch & Co. grocery warehouse

Is: Reid-Murdoch Building (Home to Encyclopeaedia Britannica, Whirlpool, Friedman Properties, offices, and restaurants)

Location: 325 N Lasalle St.

Tip: The four clocks may look and be old, but they're accurate: In 2005, they were upgraded with precision satellite technology.

68

Sleep in the First Skyscraper to Rely on Metal and Glass

The Reliance building had a tough start—architect John Root died unexpectedly after the base of the building was completed. Left without plans, Charles Atwood took over in 1894 and designed the rest of the fourteen stories.

The World's Fair's "white city" inspired the light-colored glazed terra cotta cladding, used for the first time on a skyscraper instead of stone. *Architectural Record* magazine said the material "will make this building stand out as a conspicuous mark in the history of architecture in America." Completed in 1895, experts now point to its steel frame and wide expanses of glass as the earliest example of today's glass-curtain-walled skyscrapers.

In the early years, doctors' and dentists' offices, jewelers, milliners, dressmakers, and tailors filled the floors above Walgreens, a jeweler, and Carson Pirie Scott. By the 1940s, a lack of maintenance left the building covered in soot, with windows boarded and terra cotta cracking and covered by gaudy signs advertising wig shops and fortune teller tenants. In 1988, plans to turn it into nonprofit offices or university dorms fell through even after the Reliance appeared on a list of fourteen preservation-worthy buildings at risk of being destroyed.

In 1993, with just six tenants, including long-time fixture Karoll's menswear on the ground floor, the city bought the building despite strong City Council opposition—"this building is not worth a dime," one alderman said—Mayor Richard M. Daley pushed to restore the historic

The ground floor Atwood restaurant is named after Daniel Burnham's chief designer—the architect of the upper floors and many 1893 World's Columbian Exposition buildings (including the Museum of Science and Industry).

When the city debated restoration years after this 1963 shot, Alderman Burton Natarus said: "If we had to repair the Lincoln Memorial or Washington Monument... would anybody object to that? No. This building in Chicago is as important as that." Courtesy of Library of Congress

relic with the severely crumbling exterior. Developers' "near miracle"— *Tribune* architecture critic Blair Kamin's words—transformed it into the Hotel Burnham (Now The Alise Chicago). Opened on Oct. 1, 1999, it is a "triumph of preserving the past," said Kamin, "executed with meticulous attention to detail."

NOW IT'S...

Was: The Reliance Building

Is: The Alise, formerly Hotel Burnham

Location: 1 W Washington St., 32 N State St.

Tip: Non-guests can ask to visit the original upstairs hallways of this "living skyscraper museum"—an authentic 1895 office building.

69

Louis Sullivan's Bullseye

"At the corner, the bulge offered a choice of five arched entrances, to invite approach from all directions ..." That's how Louis Sullivan's "Queen of State Street"—universally acknowledged to be one of Sullivan's masterpieces—was described by his biographer. With three bays on Madison Street, the corner rotunda, and seven bays on State Street, the 1899 building was considered a uniquely American department store, unlike the historical European, Beaux Arts design of neighboring Marshall Field & Company.

The original retailer, Schlesinger & Mayer, sold the building early on to Carson Pirie Scott & Company.

Sullivan's steel-frame technology was used to great advantage on the horizontal store, marked by cast-iron ornament of leaves, vines, and berries on the lower two floors, topped by terra cotta–framed Chicago windows. The large display windows on the ground level offered plenty of natural lighting for the store, situated between State Street and Wabash Avenue, and Madison and Monroe Streets.

In the scrolling of the rotunda, "4"s on either side of the arches (one in reverse) are flanked by Sullivan's LHS monogram. The number may refer to 1904, the year the building was completed.

Carson's closed this location in 2007, and the building was renamed Sullivan Center, with offices and the School of the Art Institute occupying some upper floors. In 2012, Target opened CityTarget on the two bottom floors.

The company's reputation for good design was bolstered by managing to morph the historic building into a thriving discount store—without marring the famed structure. *Tribune* architecture critic Blair Kamin wrote, "It revives the building as a living landmark, not a frozen museum piece."

"The right balance between preserving the aesthetic integrity of one of the nation's great works of architecture and projecting the visual brand of one of the nation's biggest retailers," Blair Kamin in the *Tribune*.

At the city's center, on the corner of State and Madison Streets, stands Louis Sullivan's masterpiece, here in 1907, not long after completion. Courtesy of Library of Congress

Inset: Designs imbedded in the red perforated metal screens were created by combining Target's logo with photos of Sullivan's rotunda ironwork. Sullivan, who believed architecture had value in everyday lives, would appreciate the combination. What's more everyday than Target? Courtesy of Joni Hirsch Blackman

The bullseye logo that seems to float in the glass corner is the only way to tell it's a Target, unless the red screens of perforated metal hanging in the windows along State and Madison are carefully examined. From the retailer that pioneered modern design: Another bullseye.

NOW IT'S...

Was: Schlesinger & Mayer; Carson, Pirie Scott & Company.

Is: CityTarget

Location: 1 S State St.

Tip: From the far northeast corner of the second floor, shoppers can look out the window at the L passing by.

When You're Out of Schlitz Tied-Houses . . . You're Out of Beer

A "Tied House" is a bar built and operated by a brewery that then offered only that company's products. The original storefront has been replaced by glass and aluminum on the first level, but the second floor exterior looks much as it always has. Hard to imagine in this craft beer era, but in the 1890s the arrangement assured brewers of loyal sales outlets. Deep-pocketed brewers selected prime real estate and constructed higher-quality buildings—many with a similar "look"—than independent saloon owners. The styles attracted customers and upgraded the image of taverns at a time when opposition to alcohol was growing.

Schlitz built fifty-seven tied houses in Chicago, more than any other brewery. Those remaining include Englewood, Wicker Park, Lake View, Uptown, Roscoe Village, McKinley Park, and Pullman.

Tied houses were often built in working class neighborhoods with nearby industrial complexes. All feature the distinctive belted-globe Schlitz logo—first seen at Schlitz's display at the 1893 World's Columbian Exposition. Many have an alternating red-and-cream face brick.

A prominent turret marks the Uptown tied house that became known as Winona Gardens, a destination for actors working at the nearby Essanay Studios. McKinley Park's tied-house is topped by a conical "witch's hat" roof. Wicker Park's is considered "one of the best-remaining examples of the tied-house system in Chicago," according to the city's landmark commission nomination, while Lake View's is "one of the most elaborate and best known."

On the edge of the "dry" industrial company town of Pullman, Schlitz

In 1890, forty-nine gallons of beer per capita was enjoyed in Chicago, more than double the statistic for residents of "beer capital" Germany, according to the *Saloon Keeper's Journal*.

You can't miss the corner turret, topped as it is with a "witch's hat" roof. The original storefront has been replaced by glass and aluminum on the first level, but the second floor exterior looks much as it always has. The Schlitz globe is on the 35th Street side. Courtesy of Illinois Historic Preservation Agency

built a complex catering to the sobriety alternative. The two-block "Schlitz Row" had three tied-houses, housing for brewery managers, and a stable for horses and carriages that delivered products to tied houses throughout the city. The stable features terra-cotta horse-head sculptures.

By 1893, about half of Chicago's seven thousand saloons were tied houses. Approximately forty remain, including those built by other Milwaukee-based brewers.

Tied houses exponentially increased the number of bars, noted a 1906 *Tribune* article: "Wherever one [brewing company] started a saloon to sell his beer exclusively, his rivals felt constrained to start saloons of their own. The result has been a costly multiplication of drinking places."

Pub proliferation attracted attention from reformers, such as the Women's Christian Temperance Union, which noted the city's bars "would form a stretch of saloons ten miles long" if placed side by side. A nineteenth century bar crawl anyone?

NOW IT'S...

Was: Schlitz Brewery Tied Houses

Is/Location:

2000 W Armitage Ave. - Dentist and "Team vs. Time" escape

1944 N Oakley Ave. - (1898) Floyd's Pub

3456 S Western Ave. (1899) One Stop Market

11400 S Front Ave. (1906) Residential

1801 W Division St. (1900-1901) Mac's American Pub

3325 N Southport Ave. (1898)- Southport Lanes

2159 W Belmont Ave. (1903) Starbucks

3159 N Southport Ave. (1903 - 1904) Schuba's Tavern

5120 N Broadway (1904) South-East Asia Center

958 W 69th St. (1898) - Caribbean Bar (may be closed)

Schlitz Brewery Stable Building 11314 S Front Ave. (1906)—Argus Brewery

Tip: Other brewers' tied houses: the Standard, 2359 S Western; Peter Hand, 1059 N Wolcott; Blatz, 835 N Wolcott, and Stege, 2658 W 24th St.

Left: The former tied-house at 1944 N. Oakley Ave. is now Floyd's Pub. The belted globe is on the Armitage Avenue side, in painted terra-cotta. The roof on the structure is a "bonnet" roof; the details around the bay are pressed metal. Courtesy of Illinois Historic Preservation Agency

Right: 11400 S. Front Ave. was constructed in 1906, part of a less-ornate complex funded by Schlitz, located across the tracks from Pullman. Just a few buildings remain in this "vice district" of saloons, housing and retail outside the dry company town. The former stable, just a block north, features horse heads in its facade. Courtesy of Illinois Historic Preservation Agency

Left: Built in 1901, this is one of the best-remaining examples of the tied-house system in Chicago. Courtesy of Illinois Historic Preservation Agency

Right: Mac's American Pub is a popular bar even today. Courtesy of Paul Hirsch Photography

Deja Booze

Just two are left, but Prussian immigrant Peter Schoenhofen built 17 buildings for his Schoenhofen Brewery when Chicago was the country's sixth largest beer producer. With his original partner, Matheus Gottfried, Schoenhofen in 1860 opened a brewery at 12th and Jefferson Streets just nine years after he arrived in America. Within two years they built this new brewery at 19th Street, and Canalport Avenue. Not long after, Gottfried sold his shares to Schoenhofen, who ran the brewery until he died in 1893.

The Administration Building, completed in 1886, was converted to offices in 2006. The powerhouse, built in 1902 to house the power plant and store hops, is notable for its tower and arched main entrance—above the archway the words "P. Schoenhofen Brewing Co." are raised in stone. In 1904, Schoenhofen employees were guaranteed six quarts of free beer "in six installments" per day, more than many other breweries.

Though built for mundane uses, the powerhouse's unusual decorative brickwork was praised in the March 1905 issue of *Architectural Record*: "No school of architecture can teach a man how to design such buildings as this brewery."

Schoenhofen's beer was unusual too, thanks to the 1,600-foot well dug in 1907. Early ads refer to the beer's "clean taste," used again in 1999 in a short-lived bottled-water enterprise.

During Prohibition in 1919, the brewery began making Green River soda using that same "pure artesian water." When alcohol production resumed post-Prohibition, money troubles had accumulated and Schoenhofen's family merged the company with Edelweiss brewery in 1934. The brewery closed for good in 1950.

West Loop's CH Distillery constructed a new distillery on the former brewery campus to produce vodka, gin, rum, and other specialty spirits, using the former bottling plant for storage.

A 1978 landmark designation report explaining the empty brewery buildings now seems ironic: "brewing beer is no longer a part of Chicago's diverse economy."

Shoenhofen's former bottling plant is being used as a warehouse by CH Distillery. In June 2017, CH Distillery opened a 20,000-square-foot distillery built on 2.5 acres of the former brewery property. Courtesy of Library of Congress

Inset (right): CH Distillery's new main distillery room on the former brewery campus includes mash tanks and 5 fermenters. A bottling station and barrel aging room are nearby. The grain room, off to the right, holds up to 75 tons of organic grains delivered to three grain silos outside. Courtesy of CH Distillery

Inset (left): CH Distillery's 50-foot-tall vodka distillation copper column purifies and distills spirits in their new warehouse on the former brewery campus. Courtesy of CH Distillery

NOW IT'S ...

Was: Schoenhofen Brewery

What it is now: CH Distillery

Location: 1701 S Clinton St., 500 W 18th St.

Tip: The buildings became famous when Jake and Elwood drove between two of them on their way to the fictional Saint Helen of the Blessed Shroud orphanage in the 1980's film, *The Blues Brothers*.

The First Sears Tower

Founded in 1894, mail-order retailer Sears, Roebuck & Co. purchased forty-one acres on the west side in 1904. Construction began in January 1905; seven thousand workers emptied sixty freight-car loads of building materials each day, using a total of twenty-three million bricks and nearly fifteen million feet of lumber for four million square feet of facilities that would house every facet of Sears' business, from manufacturing to marketing.

Opened in 1906, the four main buildings were the Power House, the Sears Tower—which was the formal entrance to the (now demolished) Merchandise Building, the Printing/Advertising building, and the Administration building.

In 1914, the Administration Building added three floors to its original two stories. Employees entered each day through a marble lobby that remains. In the basement was one of five restaurants offering meals to the nine thousand employees. (The others included separate cafeterias for men and women.)

An Allstate Insurance Building, athletic field houses for men and women, tennis courts, and a track and field were all added later. Nearby rail lines provided elevated trains for employee commutes and freight railroads to both receive goods and ship out orders.

By the 1960s, the largest retailer in the world started planning to leave its "city" for the real one. The new 110-story Sears Tower—the tallest building in the world at the time—was constructed in the Loop in 1974, emptying most of the Lawndale campus. In 1987, even distribution ceased operating from the Merchandise Building.

Reinvented as Homan Square in the early 1990s, the campus offered community services and was filled with mixed-income, affordable single-family and two-flat homes to buy and rent. A community center was built where the Merchandise Building had been.

At fourteen stories, what's now Nichols Tower was the tallest building outside of downtown when constructed in 1906. It even had an observation deck.

The former Printing facility, Administration Building and Merchandise building with the original Sears Tower on the Homan campus. Sears' first retail store opened inside the Merchandise Building in 1925; the printing facility has become income-restricted apartments. Courtesy of Library of Congress

Inset: Now known as the Nichols Tower, the former Sears Tower is on the left and the Powerhouse is on the right. Courtesy of Darris Harris

The Power House was shut down in 2004; eight years later the deteriorating, vacant building found new purpose, empowering kids' lives as a 675-student, public charter high school.

NOW IT'S...

Was: Sears, Roebuck & Co. Headquarters; Power Plant

Is: Nichols Tower; DRW College Prep High School

Location: 900 S Homan Ave., 3333 W Arthington St.

Tip: Empty since 1987, the tower reopened in 2015, offering economic, educational, job, housing, and youth leadership services, along with arts programming and cultural events.

From Largest Retail Store to Enlarging Minds

Grand proportions, simple design—kind of a big deal in architecture history. The oldest surviving department store in the city helped make State Street "that Great Street." Commissioned by a former Marshall Field partner, Levi Leiter, the building was designed by William Le Baron Jenney for Siegel, Cooper & Co. The historic landmark is one of the country's most important examples of metal-frame architecture.

Leiter famously told Jenney he wanted a "great retail store, as complete and perfect in all its appointments as the resources of modern science and art can make it . . . [and]should the building not be required for a single store, it is [to be] arranged so as to be readily subdivided."

One of the "great commercial monuments" of the city, it filled the whole block from Van Buren Street to Congress Parkway with 553,000 square feet of spaciousness. Its only rival sat just down State Street—Louis Sullivan's Carson Pirie Scott store.

Leiter II (as it's known; Leiter I is gone) was "remarkable in its time," according to its landmark application. Siegel, Cooper & Co. vacated after seven years. Various enterprises leased the building until 1932, when it became Sears, Roebuck & Company's flagship store. Sears anchored the corner for more than fifty years, even buying the building in 1969 from Leiter's estate.

Leiter's extraordinarily large windows foreshadowed today's glass-dominated structures. All that light was perfect to show off merchandise, while few columns interrupted the wide floor space with sixteen-foot-tall ceilings inside.

Outside, the south side facades were opened at street level for pedestrians during the widening of Congress Street in the 1950s.

When the "Father of the skyscraper" designed this 1891 building, it was the largest retail store in the world. The famous riveted metal frame runs along the exterior above the first floor.

This undated postcard was created between 1891 to 1898, when the building was a Siegel, Cooper & Co. department store. Architect William Le Baron Jenney constructed bridges for the Union Army in the Civl War before pioneering steel-frame construction. Courtesy of V. O. Hammon Publishing Company

Inset: Here in 1963, but Sears reigned on State Street from 1932 through 1986. It remains, as its landmark nomination noted, "undeniably a monument on State Street, just as Levi Leiter had intended." Courtesy of Library of Congress

Remodeling by Sears and Robert Morris College, which moved there in 1998, has changed most of the interior but staircases in the building's center retain the original ornamental grillwork. Those here for higher education also shouldn't miss the historic elevator doors on their way up.

NOW IT'S . . .

Was: Siegel, Cooper & Co., Sears Roebuck & Co.

Is: Robert Morris University Center

Location: 403 S State St.

Tip: L. Z. Leiter and the year of construction (MDCCCXCI) is carved just under the cornice, high above the State Street entrance.

Gold in That (Former) Factory

It was 1891 when Charles Alexander Smith, whose piano manufacturing business at Indiana and Franklin Streets was growing rapidly, bought a site on Clybourn Avenue to build a larger plant. Smith and a new partner, G.K. Barnes, acquired the Strohber Piano Co. in 1906, and by 1913 they needed even more space—adding a large tract of vacant land southwest of their property. Smith, Barnes & Strohber was among the leading player-piano manufacturers in the country.

SBS was acquired in 1924 by Continental Piano; the factory was sold in 1926 for $150,000 to James B. Day Co., which manufactured shellacs, lacquers, enamels, stains, and floor wax in the six-story factory for decades. At the time of the sale, the *Tribune* noted "an eight-car switch track of the Chicago, Milwaukee & St. Paul railway serves the property, providing excellent transportation facilities. It is also located close to street car and elevated railway transportation."

In 1964, Day moved to Carpentersville; the factory was purchased by Gold Eagle Products Co., which blended automotive additives there for the next twenty years. Ready to move to a larger facility in 1983, Gold Eagle principals Robert and Richard Hirsch were surprised to learn their Clybourn buyer, Tem Horowitz, imagined fifty-seven loft-style condominium units in their decidedly-not-luxurious, century-old factory with fourteen- and sixteen-foot ceilings. Guess they hadn't noticed the later-advertised "stunning views."

"It was a heavy timber loft building with brick walls, outbuildings, and vacant land, nicely located on the fringe of Lincoln Park at the time. It was an industrial wasteland. People were skeptical, but it sold out immediately," said eagle-eyed developer Horowitz, as if his words were scored with piano music from the factory's past. "To my mind, it was an opportunity, one of

A 1990 *Tribune* article reported: "They gutted it, replacing the mechanical systems, adding a steel superstructure. In 1984, they put it up for sale. Most bankers and real estate people thought it was a sure loser."

With the John Hancock Building in the distance, this photo is from 1969 or so, when Gold Eagle's logo adorned a later-removed water tower. The "outbuildings" on the right were turned into three townhouses. Courtesy of Bill Gurolnick

Inset: Architects Pappageorge Haymes' renovation was completed in 1984. Developer Harry Huzenis said the project had "had an impact on the Sheffield area, sort of gave it a backdrop, expanded the parameters." Courtesy of Joni Hirsch Blackman

the first complete loft projects anywhere."

No arguments these days—the place is still golden.

NOW IT'S...

Was: Smith, Barnes & Strohber Piano factory, James B. Day & Company, Gold Eagle Company.

Is: Clybourn Lofts, condos and townhomes

Location: 1872 N Clybourn Ave.

Tip: The author spent countless hours here, playing on typewriters, riding the freight elevator, and watching filling lines in the 1960s and 1970s.

Mending Civil War Vets

The Chicago building with perhaps the longest history began with an 1863 public newspaper appeal soliciting donations to build a permanent home for disabled Union Army soldiers. The previous, rented soldiers' home "cannot accommodate comfortably one in ten who apply." Women's groups organized fundraisers and went door to door to raise money for the "Soldier's Rest" to be built along Lake Michigan by Camp Douglas—a Civil War training and prison camp.

"It was . . . the imperative duty of the people to care for these maimed ones to the end . . . the ladies set about the raising of funds wherewith to build a permanent Home," the *Tribune* reported in May, 1866.

Soldiers' homes were common across the country in those days as hotels for servicemen passing through town, often later becoming veterans' nursing or retirement homes. The *Tribune* applauded the Soldier's Home, opening that May, for "the care of veterans whose frames have been so wayworn in the successful struggle for the maintenance of the union as to render them incapable of self-support . . . A full company of heroes were there . . . admiring its many provisions for their comfort, their hearts brimful of gratitude."

The four-story building featured a porch positioned for lake breezes. It provided services for "blind, crippled and maimed residents . . . more coming all the time." Because of its south side location, the Rest escaped the Great Fire. It was designed by the same architect (William Boyington) who designed the Water Tower, which famously also escaped the Fire.

After the war, the convalescent home became a permanent residence for disabled Union Army veterans, often providing them a place to live out their lives.

"A resting place for those who return to us from the battle field—ruined in health, crippled for life, and, but for us, friendless and homeless," reported the *Chicago Tribune*, 1863.

In an 1863 *Chicago Tribune* article, it was noted that the home "gradually changed from ... a resting place of your soldiers going to and from the field of battle to one for sick and disabled soldiers ... without money and without friends." Courtesy of Illinois Historical Preservation Agency

Inset: JNKA Architects' 2009 renovation included restoring four original portions of the building and constructing an administration center where non-historic additions had been. Courtesy of JNKA Architects

The Sisters of St. Joseph of Carondolet purchased Soldier's Home and Rest in 1872 to replace the St. Joseph Orphan Asylum that burned down in the previous year's fire. For more than one hundred years it was an orphanage, and later, a home for dependent, disturbed children.

In 2008, the Catholic Church turned it into offices for seventeen Archdiocesan agencies, restoring the exterior to its full glory.

NOW IT'S ...

Was: Soldier's Home and Rest

Is: Archdiocese of Chicago's Cardinal Meyer Center

Location: 739 E 35th St.

Tip: The Italianate-style structure is the only surviving building in Chicago associated with the Civil War.

White (House) Wedding

Where Lake Michigan meets 71st Street, 300 of the city's elite built the palace-like South Shore Country Club in 1906. The exclusive, restrictive private club sat on 64.5 acres. So popular, Chicago's largest private golf club needed a waitlist for potential members in 1953; membership peaked at 2,200 in 1957. But when members fled the south side to join newer suburban clubs, 1963's membership had fallen to 1,370. A 1967 decision to uphold its decades-long ban on Jews and African Americans virtually sealed its death sentence. With membership dipping to 731 and the deficit at $177,000, the deteriorating club was abandoned in 1973.

Purchased by the Chicago Park District for $10 million, plans were floated to demolish the clubhouse in favor of a cinder block field house. The Park District Superintendent's announcement that the historic, opulent facility wasn't needed "down there" sparked opposition rallies and formation of a coalition of arts organizations, preservationists, and community groups. Ironically, the diverse coalition that lobbied to save the club included many who'd been banned from membership since its inception. Their activism convinced the Park District to withdraw its demolition request in 1978 and renovate the main clubhouse into a major cultural center offering professional performances, exhibits, arts-oriented education, and leisure activities for the community.

A 1984 restoration into "The Gem of the Southside" transformed it into one of the Park District's most significant historical sites, featuring a nine-hole golf course that may partner with Jackson Park's nine-hole course, a beach garden, and a nature center and bird sanctuary. The Chicago Police Mounted Unit has used the club stables since 1976.

The banquet facility is chosen by many for wedding rreceptions. This included, in 1992, a young couple then known as Michelle Robinson and Barack Obama.

Architects Marshall and Fox also designed the Drake and Blackstone hotels. The only remaining portion of the original structure is the ballroom (now Paul Robeson Theatre) on the south end.

A 1943 postcard shows the two-faceted charms of the South Shore club—a golf course to the west, Lake Michigan to the east. Courtesy of Curt Teich & Co.

Inset: The grand ballroom was connected to a huge dining room by a wide corridor. Club guests included stars such as Bing Crosby and Jean Harlow, philosopher and humorist Will Rogers, and aviator Amelia Earhart. Courtesy of Chicagopc.info

NOW IT'S ...

Was: South Shore Country Club

Is: South Shore Cultural Center, Chicago Park District

Location: 7059 South Shore Dr.

Tip: Named after the country club's "Birdcage Club," Washburn Culinary & Hospitality Institute's on-site, upscale Parrot Cage restaurant features American cuisine.

Vaudeville and Movies Before Oprah

On land owned by the Marshall Field estate at the corner of—where else?—State and Lake Streets, this one-hundred-year-old building was built in 1917 for laughs . . . home of the Orpheum vaudeville circuit. Before long, this, one of Chicago's premier theaters, was added to RKO's movie palace chain. The Chicago Theater, designed by the same architects but more ornate, was constructed across the street a few years later.

In 1938, Balaban & Katz bought the place, continuing the live act and movies tradition. Above the theater section of this building are ten stories of offices, where television station W9XBK went on the air in 1940. The alphabet moniker changed a few times before it became WLS-TV. Where'd they get those letters? At the "World's Largest Store," Sears— owner of the station.

By 1941, the 2,649-seat State-Lake showed movies only—in its last fifteen years or so, mostly action films, until it closed on "doomsday," after the 9:30 p.m. showing of *Indiana Jones and the Temple of Doom* on June 28, 1984.

The upstairs tenant bought the place and remodeled the theater into a two-level, broadcast center (with seating for 250 audience members) — Channel 7 TV was located downstairs and its WLS-AM and FM station moved from Michigan Avenue to occupy the upstairs.

The huge neon marquee—a fixture on North State Street for nearly a century—was removed, but the exterior was beautifully restored to its 1920s applause-inspiring look.

WLS-TV in 2006 transformed the existing retail and broadcast space into a tourist attraction similar to that of New York's *Today Show*. The big windows invite the public to watch the show from State Street.

The State-Lake theater was converted the same year Oprah Winfrey arrived at WLS-TV to host A.M. Chicago in 1984, broadcasting her first namesake talk show from here in 1985.

Advertisements announced that The State-Lake Theater's policy of featuring seven vaudeville acts, alternating continuously with an exclusive first-run feature "photoplay" from 11 a.m. to 11 p.m. "inaugurated a new era in popular price entertainment ... copied in every city in the United States." (circa 1920s) Courtesy of Rene Avila

Inset: The theater that had seats for 2,800 attracted more than 70,000 patrons per week, according to the company. Courtesy of Cinema Treaures

A year and a half later, a minivan—reminiscent of those action shows—crashed through the window of the studio during the 10 o'clock news broadcast. Worse than the old pie-in-the-face smashes of Vaudeville, thankfully no one was hurt.

NOW IT'S ...

Was: Rapp and Rapp-designed State-Lake Theater

Is: Office space and headquarters for ABC-WLS TV and radio

Location: 190 N State St.

Tip: Strolling along State, stop and enjoy the live show; look for theater masks in the facade left from early theater days.

The Bank of Art

The roof literally fell in—appropriate for a structure that had housed several failed banks and had numerous connections to scandals—allowing snow and rain to nearly complete a decimation years of neglect had begun. The last vestige of a once-dense commercial area would likely have been razed. But 1923's Stony Island Trust and Savings Bank was saved by art . . . and $4.5 million.

While a financial institution, the stately twenty-thousand-square-foot building featured a dramatic vaulted banking lobby. But despite 17 attempts at redevelopment, it had been vacant since 1979. The 18th attempt hit the jackpot.

Bought from the city for $1 in 2012, artist and urban planner Theaster Gates's Rebuild Foundation—a nonprofit founded in 2010 to "foster culture and development in underinvested neighborhoods"—restored the building and is headquartered there.

Fundraising included selling one hundred marble slabs from the bank for $5,000 each—the "Bank Bonds" were the building's "last usable currency" and carried the inscription: "In ART we trust."

Though "friendly advice" encouraged Gates to "walk away," he persisted. The bank houses books and periodicals donated by John H. Johnson, publisher of *Ebony* and *Jet* magazines; art and architectural history from the University of Chicago; Edward J. Williams's "negrobilia" artifacts; and the vinyl archive of Frankie Knuckles, the "Godfather of House Music."

Part gallery, part media archive, part library, event space, and part community center since October 2015, the Arts Bank offers free arts and cultural programming. Reclamation art (Gates' passion) is everywhere, including the two-story library's reading room tables made of the rooftop water tanks' redwood.

"Projects like this require belief more than they require funding," Theaster Gates said. Proof that even in "the middle of the hood . . . great things could happen anywhere if we invest in it."

Abandoned for years when Theaster Gates first walked in, water dripped from the ceiling, the roof had a hole, and broken glass and plaster pieces littered the floor of what had been, in the 1940s and '50s, Southmoor Bank. Courtesy of WayOut Wardell

Inset: The William Gibbons Uffendell-designed building, described by Rebuild as a "sort of living room for the neighborhood," is open to the public. Courtesy of Illinois Historic Preservation Agency

The website describes "a space for neighborhood residents, as well as a destination for artists, scholars, curators, and collectors to research and engage with South Side history."

History came to life on Oct. 9, 2016 at a fundraiser for U.S. Senator Tammy Duckworth's campaign—the headliner was familiar with rescuing financial collapses: Then-president Barack Obama.

NOW IT'S...

Was: Stony Island Trust and Savings Bank, Stony Island State Savings Bank, Southmoor Bank and Trust, Guaranty Bank and Trust

Is: Stony Island Arts Bank

Location: 6760 S Stony Island Ave.

Tip: Deliberately unrestored details—the bank vault with rusted safe deposit boxes and adding machines—help visitors grasp the resurrection's extent.

Screwdrivers and All That Jazz

A chapter of Chicago's legendary jazz history can be traced to this former automobile repair/storage garage and former hardware store, the premier building that remains, which was once associated with Chicago jazz in the 1920s and 1930s. The Sunset Cafe's reputation as the city's hottest jazz club grew quickly. It was considered the home of the "Chicago sound," featuring the city's best musicians.

The house band was often accompanied by Louis Armstrong on the trumpet and Earl "Fatha" Hines on the piano. Armstrong's "Sunset Cafe Stomp" is named after the club where his star began to rise. Sunset was considered a second home for Count Basie and is the place where Cab Calloway got his start. Other young artists who began their careers at Sunset jam sessions include Benny Goodman and Jimmy Dorsey.

Performances often were accompanied by floor shows that introduced Chicago audiences to the latest dances. In 1937, it was remodeled—a mural depicting musical themes was added—and became the new home for the relocated Grand Terrace Cafe.

Grand Terrace closed in 1950 and then the building housed local Democratic committee offices. In the 1960s, the Bronzeville building was sold by Louis Armstrong's manager, Joe Glaser, to David Meyer's grandfather, who transformed it into a hardware store. Meyer's Ace Hardware was often visited by jazz aficionados who wanted to see the historic jazz mural in the back office, or musicians who wanted a chance to play on the old stage.

But the highest measure of the building's importance may have come in a 2001 *New York Times* story about an amazing find of "lost" recordings

"You're standing on holy, sacred ground," jazz musicians would tell hardware store owner David Meyers when they visited the former club. "I autographed plungers for people all the time."

The Sunset Cafe opened on Aug. 3, 1921 and was owned by Edward Fox and Sam Dreyfus, said jazz expert Phil Pospychala. The club was one of the most popular on the South Side, drawing musicians from all over the city to hear performers like legendary singer/trumpeter Louis Armstrong. Courtesy of David Meyers

Inset: Even after closing the hardware store his family had owned for 55 years, David Meyers agreed to host jazz concerts in the emptying space. Courtesy of Joni Hirsch Blackman

by young Johnny Cash, Patsy Cline, and George Jones, a discovery called "unprecedented in country music."

"They are the equivalent of someone finding pristine-sounding recordings of Louis Armstrong and King Oliver playing at the Sunset Cafe in Chicago."

NOW IT'S...

Was: Sunset Cafe

Is: Meyers Ace Hardware

Location: 315 E 35th St.

Tip: The hardware was sold in February 2017; the new owner said he may restore the murals and offer access to them.

Musical Building, Melodic Street

Constructed in 1896, this ornate building has always been filled with music. Originally a beer and dance hall frequented by local German immigrants, it was built with "public hall" rental space for meeting rooms on the second floor. Over the years, The Aldine (aka Aldine Hall) was used by fraternal and civic groups, as well as for banquets and weddings. Like many nearby buildings, first-floor commercial space was topped with upper-floor apartments.

Old Town School of Music since 1968, it's one of the most recognizable buildings along a landmarked stretch of Armitage (from Racine Avenue and Halsted Street along the former "Center Street") that's chock full of turn-of-the-century gems with picturesque architectural detailing. Constructed mostly between 1870 and 1930, developers favored the pressed-metal-decorated commercial buildings with visually appealing bays, cornices, and corner turrets to attract tenants interested in capitalizing on the new elevated train station, which replaced the old horse-drawn streetcars.

Armitage was the neighborhood's main commercial area in those years, with working-class homes built to the north and the south. Many similar neighborhood shopping streets built during Chicago's boom years have been destroyed or remodeled beyond recognition.

This western section of Lincoln Park was rural until the Chicago Fire when neighborhoods to the east were destroyed. Not a bad reason to drink and dance at the Aldine.

"One of the finest remaining nineteenth-century neighborhood commercial streetscapes," the Victorian-era buildings offer "an excellent feel for the intimate scale, visual eclecticism and beauty" of period shopping districts: according to the city's Landmark Designation report.

Most of the buildings on this stretch of the historic district combine first-floor stores with upper floor apartments. The view is often enjoyed by riders of the various L lines that pass through the Armitage station. Courtesy of Old Town School of Folk Music

Inset: The Old Town School of Folk Music moved to the former Aldine Halls and Tavern in 1968. The former banquet and wedding space had family quarters upstairs that were converted to offices, while the halls became classrooms. Courtesy of Old Town School of Folk Music

NOW IT'S...

Was: The Aldine public hall

Is: Old Town School of Music's Children's building

Location: 909 W Armitage Ave.—(Armitage between Halsted Street and Racine Avenue)

Tip: Originally "Sheffield's Addition to Chicago," the area was named for leading property owner Joseph Sheffield, who ran the local plant nursery.

Fashioned after a New York Men's Store

"Plans call for a building of Old English design, something Chicago architects seem to have overlooked for Loop skyscraper design," said the December 1926 announcement.

It lived up to the vision—a stone, gothic-style base is topped by a Tudor half-timbered stucco-and-wood upper level projecting gable, with an unusual octagonal corner copper turret on the west side.

The first five of 15 floors were originally home of The Finchley Company, a New York men's clothing manufacturer. Company offices, as well as various specialty clothing stores and dental offices, were located above.

The first hint of trouble for the fashionable store came in 1961, the year its New York store closed. The National Sporting Goods Association bought 23 E Jackson, originally to turn it into a sporting goods merchandise mart and eventually to provide showroom space to members for "year-long display." Finchley's remained in the six lower floors until July 1963, when it became the victim of a "new era in selling," company spokesman, Jerry Verlen said, fifty years before similar sweeping change—online stores—again affected retail stores.

"Changes in men's apparel retailing have made the store an anachronism," said Verlen. "The store, patterned after the slow and relaxed English way of selling, fails to meet the requirements of today's fast-moving society."

In 1972, The Finchley Building was sold to DePaul for $1.2 million. Noting how "new buildings nearby," such as the Sears Tower and Standard Oil of Indiana, would likely increase the number of downtown businesspeople, DePaul president Rev. John R. Cortelyou selected Finchley because of the close relationship of the university's colleges of law and commerce to Chicago's business community.

Architect Alfred Alschuler of Chicago was directed to replicate Beverly S. King's New York Finchley store, built at Fifth Avenue and 46th Street in 1924.

This 1958 photo of the top six floors of the former Finchley building was taken for architects Friedman, Alschuler & Sincere. Courtesy of Chicago History Museum

Inset: DePaul University renamed the building Comerford J. O'Malley Place in honor of the Vincentian philosophy professor who was also dean of the College of Commerce and University president. Courtesy of DePaul University/Jeff Carrion

Renamed in 1980 to honor former chancellor and president, the Rev. Comerford J. O'Malley Law School occupies the upper floors—grooming the very type of professionals who once shopped at Finchley's.

NOW IT'S...

Was: The Finchley, a New York-based men's clothing store

Is: DePaul University's O'Malley Place; Pazzo's Cucina Italiano

Location: 23 E Jackson Blvd.

Tip: The O'Malley building (and Lewis Center next door) were both evacuated the morning of April 13 during the city's flood of 1992.

Deep Dive on Deep Dish

The mansion at what was known as No. 292 Ohio in the late 1890s and early 1900s belonged to Mr. and Mrs. Jonathan Slade. By 1943, the lower floor of the Victorian home had been transformed into a brand-new type of Chicago restaurant. "The Pizzeria" wasn't the first pizza joint in town, just the most unusual. Italy native Ric Riccardo, owner of Riccardo's Restaurant, and liquor distributor Ike Sewell liked traditional, lighter Italian pizza, but put a Chicago spin on it—deeper, heavier, crunchier, and with the sauce on top of the cheese.

Within a few years, they changed the restaurant's name to Pizzeria Riccardo (not that customers cared). The dense, deep-dish pie was delicious and popular, no matter what the moniker. Crowds necessitated the pair open another pizzeria in another mansion down the street in 1955. Calling that one "Pizzeria Due," they logically decided to change the name of the first to "Pizzeria Uno."

Apparently Riccardo's one-time bartender, Adolpho "Rudy" Malnati, Sr. also lived in upper-floor apartments at 29 E Ohio, according to 1950s phone books. Malnati was the manager of Pizzeria Riccardo and may also have eventually become a co-owner.

If his name sounds familiar, it should. His son, Luciano "Lou" Malnati—manager of Pizzeria Due in 1955—founded another popular Chicago pizza chain in 1971. Uno cook Alice Mae Redmond went on to create Gino's East. Rudy Malnati's wife made pizza dough at Pizano's Pizza, founded in 1991 by their son, Rudy, Jr. Easy as pie to see how Chicago's pizza preoccupation expanded outward from that one corner.

The only true substitute for Pizzeria Uno, however, is Pizzeria Due—serving exactly the same pizza in a different vintage mansion.

Just a block away at 619 N Wabash is Pizzeria Due, located in the former mansion of lumber magnate Nathan Mears, whose daughter's former home is now Pizzeria Uno.

A 1943 newspaper article hanging on Uno's wall ends with this now amusing question: "Will Mr. (Ike) Sewell's deep dish pizza catch on here in Chicago?" Courtesy of Pizzeria Uno

NOW IT'S ...

Was: Mr. and Mrs. Jonathan Slade's home

Is: Pizzeria Uno

Location: 29 E Ohio St.

Tip: The all-original pizzeria with a tin ceiling is nothing like the chain version and so popular, there's often a wait.

Unique Arts (& Crafts)

The nation's oldest surviving artists' studio was built in the backyard—behind the stables—of benefactor Judge Lambert Tree's mansion at Wabash and Ontario. Though his home was razed in 1910 (replaced by the Medinah Temple) his legacy, Tree Studios, remains. Tree and his wife Anna wanted artists to remain in Chicago after attending and/or displaying work at the 1893 World's Fair. Historians note the studios played "an important and ongoing role in the art and culture of Chicago and of the nation."

The unique 1894 structure offered studios for rent to artists, subsidized by the retail cast-iron storefronts along State Street on the ground floor. Though the original 50 loft-studios were created as workspaces, artists eventually moved in.

Interaction between artists was encouraged with connecting doors between studios, and hallway display cases housed residents' work. The interior courtyard for concerts and gatherings, served as an oasis of culture in the young city.

The continual waiting list of artists wanting high-quality studio space prompted construction of two annexes after Tree's 1910 death—one along Ohio Street in 1912 and another along Ontario Street in 1913. Though the original structure is Queen Anne style, the annexes are considered one of Chicago's best examples of English Arts & Crafts, a brick chimney and a carving of an artist's palette.

Tree Studios offers a rare look into what Chicago buildings looked like just before the turn of the century, when residents like J. Allen St. John, illustrator of the *Tarzan* books, and John Stoors, sculptor of the statue of Ceres atop the Chicago Board of Trade building, were tenants. The landmark designation was definitive: "There simply are no other buildings like it, in Chicago or elsewhere in the U.S."

"Chicago can at last boast of a studio building, wherein the artist may have as many comforts as his more favored brother the office man," stated *The Arts* magazine in March 1895.

Designed by Parfitt Brothers, and the annexes by Hill and Woltersdorf, Tree Studios' exterior features a Longfellow poem as timeless as the buildings themselves: "Art is long, Time is fleeting; So be up and doing, still achieving, still pursuing." Courtesy of Friedman Properties

Inset: The Art Institute's dean in 1980 said the studios represented "A combination of economic and cultural activity that very few other buildings have been able to achieve in Chicago's history." Courtesy of Friedman Properties

NOW IT'S...

Was: Lambert Tree Studios

Is: Tree Studios, offices for painters, architects, fashion and interior designers, graphic artists, and a photographer.

Location: 4 E Ohio/5 E Ontario/603-621 N State St.

Tip: Along Ontario, visitors can find "Studio Building" carved above a doorway. The faces of Lambert and Anna Tree are carved on either side.

Sharp Condos

When a complex is named "Pencil Factory," it better be a place where lead writing utensils were created. Proof is carved in stone—pencil tips are sculpted in terra cotta reliefs along the top of the building.

Built in 1917, the former Wahl Adding Machine Co. made its adding machines, pens, and "Eversharp" pencils there. Demand for the pencils was so strong in 1920, the *Chicago Tribune* announced construction of a four-story, 150,000 square-foot addition. Three years later, owner John C. Wahl was identified as "head of the Eversharp Pencil Co." (The pencils apparently got together and erased the adding machines.)

During World War II, manufacturing shifted into high gear—1,800 employees worked two shifts to fulfill a contract to produce pencils and newly invented ballpoint pens for the Army and Navy.

Several newsworthy situations happened in the factory. In 1926, in what sounds like a scene from an old movie, "eight masked bandits" armed with guns and dynamite entered, "bound and gagged three night employees, blew a half a dozen safes and escaped five hours later with loot amounting to $25,000 in gold and gold pen points." The company routinely kept on the premises as much as $150,000 worth of gold used to make pen points.

In 1937, the city's first industrial sit-down strike against a private business was staged by the Wahl-Eversharp Pen Company's 150 employees. In 1963, six sticks of dynamite were found fastened to a molding machine in a plastic toy company on the third floor of the building; no mention of whether the toys had anything to do with it.

Parker Pen acquired Eversharp in 1957, moved manufacturing to Arlington Heights, and afterwards various industrial tenants occupied the factory. Purchased in 1987 by developers enamored with its residential-heavy location, the building's purpose was rewritten in ink, opening in 1990 as Roscoe Village Lofts.

"While the workers made merry during the night, a rigid line of seventy-five policemen surrounded the plant, stopping all relatives and friends of the strikers who sought to pass in supplies."

The Wahl/Eversharp Company patented and manufactured the first commercially successful mechanical pencil. Courtesy of Wahl-Eversharp Catalog

Inset: The old pencil factory, designed by Bernard H. Prack, was a natural to reinvent as residences because of its un-factory-like location on a tree-lined residential street. Courtesy of Joni Hirsch Blackman

NOW IT'S...

Was: Eversharp Pencil Co.

Is: Pencil Factory Lofts

Location: 1800 W Roscoe St.

Tip: Seriously ever-sharp: the pencil company manufactured safety razors for a while; one of the last major tenants was a syringe maker.

Walt Disney's First "World"

That wish for Disneyland that Walt's heart made? It may have been dreamed by him while sleeping in the Chicago neighborhood where his carpenter dad, Elias Disney, built their house in 1892.

Elias and Flora, with sons Herbert and Raymond, moved into the 18 × 28-foot wood structure in early 1893; Roy was born later that year. Drawn to Chicago because Elias' brother, Robert, lived and worked here—part of a construction crew for a hotel near the site of the 1893 Columbian Exposition—Elias found work as a carpenter at the fair's Midway Plaisance pavilions in Jackson Park.

(Could his dad's stories of working near the White City at the World's Fair have influenced Walt's dreams? Biographers disagree. Jiminy Cricket hasn't commented.)

On a salary of just $1 a day, Elias saved enough to start his own home-building business, following the same pattern: he bought the land, Flora (good with a sketch pad!) drew up the plans.

Fourth son Walter Elias was born in a second-floor bedroom eight years after Roy. Their sister, Ruth, arrived almost exactly two years later, on December 6, 1903. The family sold the house and moved to Missouri in February 1906 when Walt was four.

Changing hands many times in the next 100-plus years, additions and renovations to the house were completed by each owner, leaving little connection to the man who built the "happiest place on earth," as far as Disney biographers were concerned.

But facing demolition, the Hermosa neighborhood house went on the market in 2013. A Los Angeles couple bought, saved it, and worked toward completing what every Disney story needs: a happy ending.

Brent Young and Dina Benadon's nonprofit company has (with the help of $250,000 donation from the Walt Disney Co.) been restoring the

The Disneys returned in 1917 when Walt was a teenager, to Chicago's North Lawndale neighborhood. His only formal art training was at the now-defunct Chicago Academy of Fine Arts.

Elias Disney bought a residential lot on Tripp Avenue on Oct. 31, 1891. A year later, he built a two-story, 18x28-foot wood cottage for $800. His younger children—Roy, Walt and Ruth—were born in the home his wife, Flora, designed. Courtesy of Walt Disney Birthplace

Inset: "We believe there's a lot of parallels between Walt and Roy's story and what kids in Hermosa go through today," Brent Young said of the project. Courtesy of Walt Disney Birthplace

home to what it looked like in 1901 in order to open it to the public. They imagine a multimedia attraction where visitors can experience what life was like for the Disneys while living there.

An early childhood creativity center is also planned—a place to inspire the children Walt spent his life entertaining.

NOW IT'S...

Was: Young Walt Disney's Home

Is: The Walt Disney Birthplace & Museum (Opening in 2017/2018)

Location: 2156 N Tripp Ave.

Tip: Elias invested in Chicago fruit drink company O-Zell Soda Co. in 1917; resurrected online @ o-zell.co

Built for Water, Great Fire Didn't Harm It

Why a castle? Maybe because Chicagoans "rejoiced" about finally quenching their thirst with clean drinking water. The so-called "flamboyant piece of plumbing" was conceived to hide a three-foot-wide, 138-foot-tall iron standpipe.

On March 23, 1867, the *Chicago Tribune* applauded "[t]he supplying of pure water to the citizens in place of the miserable filth miscalled water with which we have been served for years past." Water finally fit for kings to drink apparently needed a crown.

Clean water, the *Tribune* predicted, "will abolish one extensive excuse for tippling whereat the temperance people will be exceedingly glad. When urging the claims of pure cold water to the patronage of the people, they have many a time and oft been met with the question . . . 'You would not have me drink our filthy water, would you?'" That argument truly held water.

The prospect of clean water was so thrilling, the tower's corner stone was laid as the cumulation of a parade. The water arrived through a tunnel dug nearly two miles offshore to an octagonal intake crib in Lake Michigan, completed the same year. Fresh water from the lake's "pure and limpid portions," was pumped through a station on what is now the opposite side of Michigan Avenue. The original pumps were plagued by vast fluctuations in water pressure, so the standpipe was added in 1869 to stabilize pressure surges throughout the neighborhood. The pipe was removed in 1906 after electric water pumps made it obsolete.

Constructed with yellowish Joliet/Lemont limestone, residents' affection for the tower was immediate and steadfast. After the Great Chicago Fire of 1871, the water tower and pumping station were the only buildings in the burned district to survive. The 154-foot-tall tower served as a functional landmark on the empty landscape the morning after the fire when "hundreds of refugees returned to the city and had nowhere else to look for bearings."

Oscar Wilde once called it a "castellated monstrosity with pepper boxes stuck all over it," and questioned why anyone would design a water tower to "masquerade as a miniature medieval castle."

The William W. Boyington-designed tower's 18th story observation deck is accessed via a spiral staircase that wraps around the 3-foot-wide 138-foot standpipe, but it hasn't been open to the public for years. Courtesy of Library of Congress

Inset: A City Gallery with rotating art exhibits is inside the tower, open 10-6:30 daily. Two drinking fountains with carved-stone lion heads are built into the walls, near the 1864 limestone dedication plaque. An exterior plaque notes "it stands as a principal memorial of 1871's great fire." Courtesy of Jim Bartholomew

Attempts to raze the tower include 1906, 1918 (when Michigan was widened, but the street was diverted around the tower instead)—and 1948. All were thwarted by adamant residents. Clean water's value apparently flowed into residents' attachment to the limestone landmark itself.

NOW IT'S...

Was: Water Tower

Is: City Gallery

Location: 806 N Michigan Ave.

Tip: Open daily, admission is free to the tower/art gallery (showcasing local photographers and artists) within "Jane M. Byrne Plaza."

Home of the 2016 World Series Champs

A few old seminary buildings at the corner of Clark and Addison were torn down in February 1914 to make way for the new Weeghman Park, which opened on April 23. The one-level fourteen-thousand-seat ballpark cost $250,000 and was home to the Chicago Federals, who played in the brand-new Federal League.

Owner Charles Weeghman, a local lunch counter magnate, took out a quarter-page ad in every Chicago newspaper: "This great park, dedicated to clean sport and the furtherance of our national game is yours, not ours. Its destiny is in your hands." He couldn't know just how beloved the place would become.

His steel-and-concrete park featured a curved-roofed grandstand with bleachers along first and third baselines and in right field, easily outshining the dilapidated West Side Grounds where the Cubs had played up until then. Chi-Feds fans paid 50 cents for bleacher seats, 75 cents for grandstand and a a dollar for box seats. It was the first ballpark to offer concession stands and employees who cleaned the stadium daily.

A Wrigley tradition started on the day the park opened: When thousands of fans couldn't get into the sold-out game, they watched from rooftops along Sheffield and Waveland.

The Whales (after a year-two name change) won the pennant their second season, but it was the league's last. When the Federal League folded, Weeghman, William Wrigley Jr., and nine other businessmen bought Chicago's National League team, the Cubs, from Cincinnati publisher Charles P. Taft for $500,000. He moved them to Weeghman Field, which by 1920's opening day was called Cubs Park.

By 1921, thanks to Weeghman's financial "disorder," investor Wrigley became the team's majority owner. The grandstands were expanded, more box seats added, and the field lowered three feet in 1923. In 1926, the

The legendary Billy Goat Curse: A smelly pet goat brought to the 1945 World Series' Game 4 was kicked out. Up 2-1 in the series until then, the Cubs lost.

The opening day crowd watching the Kansas City vs. Chicago Federal League matchup at Addison & Clark Streets on April 23, 1914. Attendance was recorded as 28,436 at the just-completed ballfield. Courtesy of Library of Congress/Kaufmann & Fabry Co.

This July 1929 photo describes the location as "Cubs Park." The buildings behind the bleachers look familiar—the clothing worn by fans, not so much. Courtesy of Library of Congress/Kaufmann & Fabry Co.

re-named Wrigley Field made plans to add a second tier over the left-field grandstands. In 1928, the upper deck was added to the rest of the park.

The bleachers and iconic scoreboard arrived in 1937, the same year Ivy vines were planted by the outfield wall. A $300 million renovation, launched in 2013, had fans concerned about changes to the Friendly Confines.

The 2016 World Series win helped. Hey Chicago, whaddaya say? The old Cubs Park is and has a winner today.

NOW IT'S...

Was: Weeghman Park, Cubs Park

Is: Wrigley Field

Location: 1060 W Addison St., at Clark

Tip: The second-oldest major-league ballpark in the country, also home to Chicago's football team, the Bears, from 1921 to 1970.

A Square Meal

Chicago's Water Tower was the only structure left standing after the Great Chicago Fire, so White Castle founder Billy Ingram thought a similar castle design would make people think of permanence; the white color was meant to imply purity and cleanliness—not something people associated with fast food in those days.

This type of "programmatic architecture" served as a sort of billboard for the company, reinforcing its theme and values. The company's 16th medieval-inspired visually-distinctive building was constructed for $4,500 during the Great Depression. This is one of very few original White Castles to survive nationwide.

Number 16 is the best example in Chicago of the first national hamburger chain, founded in Wichita in 1921, and thought of as the "father" of American fast food—30 years before McDonald's. White Castle popularized a new type of burger, which previously resembled a meatball between cold slices of bread, eaten only at carnivals.

Upton Sinclair's 1906 book, *The Jungle*, had made Americans less than enthusiastic about beef. Trying to prove their ground beef was safe to eat, the founders' small restaurants emphasized cleanliness for each hamburger-preparation step.

Thinner, square meat patties with onions and warm buns were grilled in an open kitchen that customers could observe. Customers nicknamed the greasy burgers "sliders." When this location opened, the nickel hamburgers were often sold five to a bag ("Buy 'em by the Sack") for a reduced 10 cents. White Castle #16 closed in 1944.

Chef Luciano & Gourmet Chicken have occupied the building since 1982, which was for a long time unrecognizable as a former White Castle. But 80 years after it was first built, a major renovation, with help from city preservationists, restored its original look.

Looks like White Castle again, but tastes like chicken.

One of the earliest fast-food restaurants in America, this 1930s building was the city's first White Castle.

Here's what White Castle #16 looked like in the early years. Typical of "roadside" or "programmatic" architecture, it connected the look of the building with the product sold inside. Years later, deteriorating and covered in other signage, it was unrecognizable as a White Castle—until its restoration in 2010. Courtesy of Ohio History Center and White Castle

Inset: The original White Castle #16 on the west end of this building adjoins the red-brick Chef Luciano & Gourmet Chicken place. But the White Castle portion still looks like a small burger joint inside, complete with an ordering window and view into the kitchen. Courtesy of Joni Hirsch Blackman

NOW IT'S...

Was: White Castle #16

Is: Chef Luciano & Gourmet Chicken restaurant

Location: 43 E Cermak Rd., corner of Wabash and Cermak

Tip: Does a former White Castle make you hungry for White Castle? You're in luck; a real one's across the street.

Waxing Nostalgic About Springs and Beer

From beer to beer on Clybourn here. In 1908, Goetz & Flodin built its brewing equipment factory at the corner of Clybourn and Willow, though the property was reportedly purchased by the Birk Bros. Brewing Co. The William D. Gibson company bought the factory in 1916 and manufactured springs of all sizes for more than forty years before moving downstate. Turtle Wax made automotive cleaning and detailing products there until the mid-1970s.

The neighborhood—between swanky Lincoln Park and the seven-thousand-resident Cabrini Green housing project (opened in 1942)—suited the factories. But as the Clybourn corridor gentrified with condominiums in the 1980s, the old factory became "one of the most interesting industrial-to-retail conversions in Chicago history." Opened in 1989, "1800 Clybourn" was a step along the neighborhood's transformation from industrial to retail/residential.

The three-level enclosed shopping center resembled a nineteenth-century industrial village. Both ends of the former factory, including original brick foundation walls and wood pillars, were restored, while the middle was demolished for parking space. The U-shaped, heavy-timber building and six smaller structures offered "stroller friendly" ramps, popular with families moving into the area. The 187,000-square-foot "visual playground" had a three-hundred-gallon saltwater aquarium and an information booth housed in an old freight elevator, not to mention the big draw: The original Goose Island Brewery's multilevel restaurant and bar. Shops were described as "independent, unexpected, creative."

It was nothing if not unique, but it didn't last. Many stores closed in the early 1990s and the building was foreclosed on in April 1993. New

"With a hulking mahogany bar at its core serving beer made mere feet away, Goose Island was revolutionary when it opened in 1988 ... one of just three breweries in the area." January 4, 2017, *Chicago Tribune.*

Here's what it looked like after a few additions to the original 1908 factory. The tower is recognizable as the one helping to hold up the current Patagonia store, where this same photo hangs with a brief history of the property. Courtesy of chicagopc.info

Inset: The upscale, urban neighborhood is not what it used to be when the Cabrini Green housing project, which was closed and demolished between the late 1990s and 2011, was nearby. Courtesy of Joni Hirsch Blackman

owners tore out the court, leaving three detached buildings surrounded by parking lots. Goose Island's original brewpub (renovated and re-opened in 2017) was the first tenant, and the only original that remains. The former factory sprang into the 21st century with an outdoor lifestyle retail center called Clybourn Place—less unusual, but still plenty of hops.

NOW IT'S . . .

Was: The William D. Gibson Company/Turtle Wax Factory

Is: Clybourn Place, lifestyle retail center

Location: 1800 N Clybourn Ave.

Tip: Next to the first-floor elevator in the vintage-vibe Patagonia store, hangs a plaque describing the property's history.

Turned Around Literally, Then Figuratively

Though the Chicago River is still the Chicago River, it is perhaps the most transformed place in Chicago. It is the reason this city grew, drawing hundreds of thousands of people—but in return, those people and the industry they brought treated the river as a dump.

Native Americans had lived by and traveled on the river. But generations of Chicagoans avoided it like the plague on the landscape it had become. Though some in these pages marveled over deteriorating buildings brought back to exquisite life, the awe over changes along the river is at least twice as inspiring.

A May 2017 *Chicago Tribune* editorial praising two new multi-use developments planned for opposite ends of the river downtown included this sentence, anticipating its readers' first reaction: "A prime catalyst can be—don't laugh—the Chicago River."

The editorial went on, "for decades the Chicago River was a source of revulsion rather than inspiration .... It's taken decades, but the river has morphed from liability to asset."

Truer words were never written. The Chicago River's Pygmalion-like triumph simply can't be overstated. Friends of the Chicago River trace much of that change to 1979's Chicago magazine article, "Our Friendless River."

The river at that point was "truly a lost resource, rarely used for recreation and inhospitable for wildlife," according to Friends of the Chicago River (inspired name!). The article, by Robert Cassidy, outlined an action plan for the future, which helped lay the foundation for the Friends of the River's formation.

Considering the 2016 completion of the people-magnet known as the Riverwalk, one particular piece of the 1979 action plan truly resonates: "Increased public access to the Chicago River is desirable ... People should be able to access the river without cars such as by walking, riding bikes, and

The south shore Riverwalk, from Lake Shore Drive to Lake Street, features six "rooms": The Marina Plaza, the Cove, the River Theater, the Water Plaza, the Jetty and the Boardwalk.

A coal barge at the east end of the Chicago River's main branch in about 1941. The Tribune Tower and Wrigley Building are noticeable towards the right and Wacker Drive's two levels to the left. Courtesy of Library of Congress

Inset: An aerial view of the Chicago River's only island—Goose Island, looking south circa 1960. Courtesy of Library of Congress

taking public transit. It should be a commuter trail for human-powered travel. Bike, canoe, kayak, and rowing equipment rentals should be available. Public access should include a variety of opportunities to experience nature, including bird watching, bat watching, and fishing."

Today's Chicago River is all that and more—an almost mind-boggling source of civic pride. The River, according to the city of Chicago, "has been transformed from an eyesore of our industrial past to an anchor of our neighborhoods' future."

Very simply, it used to be awful and it is now amazing. But Friends of the Chicago River deserves the last word: "It is a river whose time has come."

NOW IT'S...

Was: The Chicago River: industrial wasteland

Is: The Chicago River: a glorious place to live, work and play

Location: North Branch, South Branch, Wolf Point, Main Branch

Tip: Enjoy the river via kayaks, rental or private boats, a river cruise, or water taxi—and the McCormick Bridgehouse & Chicago River Museum

INDEX

PHOTO INDEX